OUT OF THE BLUE

Out of the Blue

Homosexuality and the Family

Martin Hallett

Hodder & Stoughton
LONDON SYDNEY AUCKLAND

First published in Great Britain 1996

The right of Martin Hallett to be identified as the Author of
the Work has been asserted by him in accordance with the
Copyright, Designs and Patents Act 1988.

10 9 8 7 6 5 4 3 2 1

British Library Cataloguing in Publication Data
A record for this book is available from the British Library

ISBN 0 340 65152 0

Printed and bound in Great Britain by
Cox & Wyman Ltd, Reading, Berks.

Hodder and Stoughton Ltd
A Division of Hodder Headline PLC
338 Euston Road
London NW1 3BH

Contents

Introduction

Feelings

It may have been quite difficult to buy this book from the bookstall or bookshop. The word 'homosexuality' is likely to provoke a strong reaction. It may be embarrassment and fear. 'What would other people think of me?' Perhaps at one time your interest in this issue would have been purely academic, but now the mention of the word 'gay' or 'lesbian' stirs up strong emotions. These may range from compassion, interest and concern to near hysteria. The issue of sexuality inevitably provokes strong emotions. The media use it all the time to do just that. Advertisers recognise that our sexuality says something about ourselves. It can often seem to be a measure of our acceptability. Sexuality is all about relationships and therefore the sexuality of someone we love will affect us. It can be wonderfully constructive and affirming, or abusive and devastating. This book may focus on the sexuality of someone close to us, but it will also relate to our own sexuality.

Aims

This book seeks to help many different people affected by homosexuality. The word 'family' is used to apply to a relative or close friend. I am seeking to help both the person affected by the homosexuality of someone else and homosexual persons themselves.

Objectivity

We cannot be truly objective when looking at an issue like this. Our own sexuality will affect the way we relate to the sexuality of somebody else. Most of us will have moral opinions on sexuality and homosexuality. My own viewpoint will be expressed. I am no more unbiased than anyone else. I will share other opinions than simply my own. Homosexuality in family and close friends is seen in many different situations. Every person is wonderfully unique and no two situations will be the same. However, there will be similarities. Some guiding principles apply to all situations and moral choices concerning homosexuality.

Fear

A crucial principle is the need to overcome fear, which is expressed in a multitude of ways, some obvious and others far more subtle. Traditionally, fear and prejudice concerning homosexuality is thought to be only in those who unthinkingly condemn homosexual people. Fear, prejudice and criticism will almost certainly provoke a response of fear. It may be vociferous and angry, or silent withdrawal and depression. We are all fearful.

The Bible says: '*There is no fear in love. But perfect love drives out fear, because fear has to do with punishment. The man who fears is not made perfect in love'* (1 John 4:18). This must be saying that we all need to work at overcoming fear and the way we do that is through loving. That can sound trite but it is wonderfully true. Overcoming fear is a lifelong experience of loving and understanding.

As a committed Christian I believe the source of complete perfect love and understanding is God the Creator. I do not have all the answers to the questions raised by the issue of homosexuality. I can only share what I have learned from my own experiences and those of other people known to me. I hope these will help if you have a son, daughter, close friend, wife, husband, father, mother, brother or sister who is homosexual – also if you are a person with homosexual feelings and want those you love to know this.

True to Life

Most situations and relationships mentioned in this book are true, given with the permission of those involved, although the names are changed. Some are true-to-life but fictitious. Although my own life and morality seek to follow the teachings of Jesus Christ, I will attempt to give a fair representation of other points of view. Some situations described will reflect the diversity of opinion. The aim is to encourage love and understanding, so healing may be experienced in lives and relationships.

The Title

Out of the Blue may describe the totally unexpected disclosure of a close friend or relative. You had no idea this person had homosexual feelings.

You may be the person sharing your homosexuality and 'coming out' relates to a sense of freedom felt having revealed a secret that made you feel unknown to others and maybe a hypocrite. At last you feel known, even if you are uncertain about the reaction of those you have told. 'Coming out' may feel more liberating than you ever imagined.

Vulnerability may not feel like freedom at all. The blues refer to sadness and depression, maybe isolation and loneliness. Perhaps coming out of the blues means much more than a dramatic change in circumstances. The long-term solution will mean understanding, accepting and working through to freedom. I hope this book will help this process, whatever your reason for reading it might be.

I want to thank all my friends and colleagues who encouraged me to produce this book. There are many special people who have loved, changed and motivated me in ways that have been healing. My own homosexuality and Christianity enable me to offer help to others through the ministry of True Freedom Trust (TfT). Since 1977 I have met thousands of people for whom homosexuality is an issue, directly or indirectly. I have learnt and am learning a lot, sometimes through my own mistakes and failures. I have hurt and been hurt in many ways with which you may identify. I have shared the pain of others in different situations. I am grateful for the support of TfT and its members, who helped me produce this book, through their stories. Special thanks to Peter and Trevor for helping me with the manuscript.

The special people in my life are also a part of this book, because they are a part of me. Thank you Jane, Nigel, Linda, Ian, Annette, Martin, Douglas and Peter. I love you very much.

1

Dreams and Nightmares

Many of us are avid fans of TV soaps. They are carefully created to be true to life, but seem to depend on the continual input of new situations and dramas, usually predictable, to keep our attention. We can be tempted to think: 'Those kinds of things just don't happen in normal everyday lives!' The truth is that they do. Sometimes our own experiences would make good soap material, even though we think they are fairly humdrum. Unlike TV soaps, they are unpredictable.

World Torn Apart

Something happens which tears our world and security apart. We ask: 'Can this really be happening to me?' People with whom we have felt close and intimate suddenly seem like strangers. Life becomes painful, with the pains of guilt, anger, frustration, maybe betrayal and helplessness. There may be a longing to try and change the situation but a feeling of total inadequacy, or a dull ache of nausea and fatigue. This is just something of the pain some people feel when a person they love reveals their homosexuality. For some the revelation is totally unexpected. For others there have been indications and amongst a lot of other emotions there is relief that at last the truth has been revealed.

Some Stories

Mark is nineteen, an only son and loved very much by his Christian parents (Pat and Richard). They were married in their thirties and longed for children. Mark's birth seemed an answer to their prayers. He grew into a handsome young man and dated a few girls but seemed to concentrate more on his academic work. This pleased Richard. Mark loves his father and mother, although he always feels a little closer to his mum. Richard often finds it difficult to express his own feelings, although he wants to show his son how much he loves him. Pat and Richard have longed for Mark to share their Christian faith, but this has not happened yet.

Mark struggled when he first went to university, but has seemed much happier over the last few months. He usually spends at least a week of his vacation at home, often accompanied by his best friend from university, Tony. At Christmas Mark was on his own, and late one evening his mum and dad noticed he seemed pensive and withdrawn. Pat asked what was the matter and Mark burst into tears. He told them he was gay and that Tony had been his partner for the last couple of months. However, Tony had started to withdraw from the relationship and Mark was feeling hurt.

Pat and Richard were stunned. They regarded themselves as fairly broadminded and although their theology was not liberal, they had always shown a lot of love and concern for homosexuals. Richard's social work and Pat's nursing career had meant many of their friends and colleagues were gay and lesbian. They always maintained that although the Bible spoke out against homosexual sex as sin, God obviously loved homosexual people.

Many feelings were swirling around in Pat's head. She desperately wanted to do something to make things better for Mark. A part of her wanted to help restore the relationship with Tony, another part felt angry with Tony for hurting her son. Yet she also wanted to make his homosexuality 'better'. She felt she should be able to take his homosexual feelings away. Her immediate reaction was to give him an aspirin and send him to bed thinking it would be all better in the morning, as if his homosexual feelings were like a sickness that she ought to be able to 'cure'. Almost as soon as that idea had gone through her mind, she dismissed it as ridiculous.

Richard also felt helpless. He longed to reach out and comfort his son, but also wanted to withdraw. Both Pat and Richard felt hurt by Mark. He seemed like a stranger. They never dreamt he could possibly have homosexual feelings. There was a silence for several minutes but the only person who noticed it was Mark. The silence was suddenly broken by Richard, who started sobbing uncontrollably. This was unusual. He grasped Mark, almost like a drowning man and they wept in each other's arms. Pat also cried, but left the men together for a moment till she joined them, her arms around them both.

Once the weeping had subsided, Mark shared the fact that he had wanted to tell them for ages. He had always felt different and found it difficult when girls had shown an interest in him to which he could not respond. His relationship with Tony had developed from a friendship into a sexual relationship when they both realised they had homosexual feelings for one another. Mark wanted to make it clear to Pat and Richard that although it had been difficult, they had not had sex in his parents' home. He respected his mum and dad's Christian beliefs, even though he did not share them. This meant a lot to Pat and Richard. When he told them this, the tears flowed again.

A few months later, the relationship between Mark and Tony was restored. Pat and Richard were still experiencing a tremendous feeling of loss. For Richard it was in the sense of losing the Mark he thought he knew and the expectancy of future grandchildren. Nevertheless he was tremendously moved by his own new-found ability to express love to his son. At one stage Pat and Richard wondered if their theology might accept Mark and Tony's relationship as a Christian one, but honestly felt this could not be so. They have been through a stage wondering if maybe God would change Mark's sexual orientation and enable him to have a heterosexual relationship. They now feel the best option is to pray for Mark and Tony's Christian conversion. They are encouraged that Mark and Tony respect their Christian beliefs, even if they do not share them.

Delroy and Rachel had been married for ten years and were in their late thirties. They had a son, Tim, aged nine, and a daughter, Sara, who was seven. Rachel had seemed distant emotionally for the past year, but Delroy thought it might be some kind of hormonal problem. They had both been active in the local pentecostal church, but Rachel's enthusiasm had waned, especially over the last few months.

One evening Rachel announced she wanted to leave Delroy and move in with another woman, Ella. Delroy was devastated. His feelings for Rachel had bordered on idolatry at times and the pain of what she told him left him feeling stunned. She asked him to respond, but he felt unable. She said she wanted to take the children. At this point, Delroy screamed: 'No! Never!' Rachel mumbled something about needing to come to some arrangement about the children and went upstairs to bed.

Over the next few days the tension became unbearable. Rachel moved in with Ella but came to visit the children each day. Delroy tried to persuade her to stay, but her response was always to say: 'I need to be true to myself at last!' Delroy worked from home and was eventually given custody of the children, although they regularly went to stay with Rachel and Ella. Rachel found this especially difficult and became bitter about it.

Several years later, Delroy remarried. Tim seemed more affected by the marriage break-up than Sara. He became very withdrawn. He seemed to blame himself for his parents' marriage breakdown at first, but Delroy and Rachel were able to talk to both their children about what had really happened. They were advised to do this together, so they would be seen to be in agreement. The children were confused by the change in Rachel's belief system, but found some of her new friends quite trendy. Their own pals generally seemed to accept the situation, although a few negative comments were made. Attitudes in their church were less positive, especially amongst the older members, including Delroy's parents. They could not understand Rachel's feelings.

Gary is twenty-five and the youngest of three children. His older brother and sister are both married. He told his parents six months ago that he was gay and their reaction at first was to blame themselves. Gary encouraged them to meet other parents in a similar situation and they found this a tremendous encouragement. They now totally accept Gary's lifestyle, although they have some fears about a few of his sexual relationships. They would like to see him settled in a stable relationship. Gary's mum and dad joined with other parents on a Gay Pride march and felt very encouraged by this. Gary's mum, Wendy, is especially keen to become more involved in fighting against discrimination towards gays and lesbians. Wendy and David (Gary's father) say they are proud to be parents of a gay son.

Gary has a network of supportive friends and is thrilled that his brother and sister also know about and accept his sexuality. The militant gay groups do not appeal to Gary, although he gets angry at some of the prejudice he knows others experience. He has become involved in HIV and AIDS work and this takes up most of his spare time.

Michael and Judith have been married for eighteen years. Michael has been aware of homosexual feelings from an early age and had a few friends who were openly gay while he was in the sixth form at grammar school. When he left school, he spent a short time working in the civil service and then joined the Royal Air Force as a military police-man. During this time he had no homosexual involvement and does not remember being particularly frustrated. He became a Christian at sixteen and felt God had called him to be in the ordained ministry. He met Judith at this time and after a short engagement they were married. At the back of his mind lay the belief that marriage would lay any homosexual tendencies to rest once and for all. Michael and Judith were advised to get married by their pastor, who said: 'I believe the Lord wants you to be married.'

For a while as a married man Michael was living a dual

lifestyle. On the one hand he was a church leader and apparently happily married. On the other he occasionally got involved in casual homosexual relationships. He went through phases of depression, and during these times of stress and anxiety would often find himself visiting places where he knew homosexuals met. It seemed more a case of seeking a sense of identity and freedom to talk about his feelings than simply sex. He felt trapped and helpless.

At one point, following a brief encounter with a young man, Michael decided he was going to walk away from his marriage and pursue a homosexual lifestyle. By this time Judith knew about his struggles and promised to stand by him as he tried to deal with them. Michael decided to stay within his marriage and soon became the leader of a new church fellowship. Several friends in the church knew about his feelings and continued to support him and Judith. The experience of seeing God use him through his struggles, rather than in spite of them, helped Michael a lot. Homosexual feelings and temptation became more integrated into his whole way of seeing himself and his relationship with God. They were not any better or worse than other struggles and temptations.

The support of his wife also helped a great deal. Judith was aware of areas in her own life with which she struggled as a Christian. Therefore Michael and Judith were able to encourage each other. They both felt much more whole and complete as people and for most of the time the homosexuality was not a major problem. Michael especially wanted to be more open within his ministry about his homosexuality, but was concerned about the reaction of his children. He feared they might be hurt if they found out about this part of their father's background from someone else. He decided he would only be open publicly about his homosexuality when he had found the opportunity to share it with his children.

His son, Adam, then sixteen, had recently become a committed Christian and was involved in his dad's church fellowship. There had been a talk at church about sexuality and this seemed to provide an opportunity for Michael to talk to Adam about his own background. He did not go into details but simply stated that it had been something of an issue in his own life. Michael encouraged his son to talk about how he felt about his father's revelations. Michael had also told Adam other personal issues related to his fears and insecurities. This transformed the father and son relationship. Adam started to be much more open with his dad about his own feelings and sexuality.

Michael and Judith were together when they talked to Gemma, then twelve, about her dad's homosexuality. It was in the context of sexual issues generally, and Gemma had already talked to her mum about sex. Adam and Gemma were not close at this time. He had been very much the 'older brother' and they each had their own circle of friends. Michael and Judith encouraged their children to talk about their feelings and reactions. A couple of mature Christians in the church, to whom Adam and Gemma related well, were also involved. Adam and Gemma knew they could talk to them in confidence if they wished.

Carol's best friend, Mary, told her one day that she was a lesbian. Mary assured Carol that she was not interested in her sexually, and at first Carol was not totally convinced. Both women were committed Christians, unmarried, in their late twenties and had known each other since they were teenagers. Carol was shocked when Mary told her and felt hurt and angry. She found it difficult to rationalise this because she knew it was not Mary's fault. There was a tremendous sense of bereavement. She felt she was experiencing a double blow. Not only had Mary told her about her lesbianism, but she had said that she felt that God would be quite happy for her to be involved in a loving lesbian relationship. This cut right through all that Carol believed, theologically. The friend with whom previously she had felt a tremendous sense of spiritual oneness now seemed a stranger.

It took Carol a long time to begin to work through all her mixed emotions. A part of her wanted to run away from the situation and abandon Mary, but another part felt strongly committed to her as a sister in Christ. Once Carol had begun to work through the sense of bereavement and accept the situation, even though she was unhappy about it, she struggled to know how she should respond as a Christian. She had no problem accepting homosexual people and their relationships, but Christians saying it was OK seemed a very different issue. Someone she knew and loved as a Christian saying it was OK seemed even more painful. Scripture verses that spoke about not having fellowship with disobedient Christians suddenly seemed frighteningly real. She now began to wonder if they applied to this situation, although part of her hoped they did not.

Mary longed for Carol to accept her new thinking and the woman, Michelle, she now described as her 'partner'. Carol felt confused. She questioned her own sexuality. Did she have sexual feelings for Mary? Was she jealous of Mary's relationship with Michelle? Should she be rethinking her own theological position? Should she have nothing more to do with Mary or Michelle? Having struggled with all these feelings and many others, Carol decided she owed it to Mary to be completely honest about the mental torment she was in. At first Mary reacted angrily, then broke down and wept.

Ultimately Carol decided she must accept Mary's situation and her viewpoint, even though she was unhappy about it. She explained to Mary that being with her in the company of her gay friends was difficult to handle. There was no problem accepting them as people, but they continually reminded her of the direction of Mary's life. Carol said this worried her so much that it hurt. She explained to Mary that it would have been completely different if Mary had not changed her theological position. She said she could try to ignore her beliefs and socialise with Mary's friends, but that would mean denying the truth of how she felt. Mary and Carol both agreed this would not be the right way forward and they both continued to meet as friends although there were many strains and barriers in the relationship because of the different directions their lives had taken. Both felt sad about this.

Gareth and Jane have two daughters and a son, all of whom are married. The eldest daughter, Sandy, had their first grandchild, Andrew, just over a year ago.

Gareth did not have a particularly good relationship with either of his parents. Up to the age of ten he was a very lonely little child. He became friendly with a boy of the same age who lived next door. They were inseparable. When they were both eleven, they started being involved with each other sexually. This continued until they drifted apart in their late teens. Gareth never identified the sexual activity as homosexuality. He became aware of strong heterosexual feelings and saw himself as thoroughly heterosexual. He married Jane when he was twenty-one. He was sometimes aware of sexual interest in boys of ten or twelve and this disturbed him. He kept these feelings to himself and never acted them out. Occasionally they came to the surface in sexual fantasies. He managed to convince himself this was not really homosexuality because it involved children rather than adults. It seemed more like a flashback to his experiences with his childhood friend.

One day Gareth was playing with a twelve-year-old boy, and during a rough and tumble game he touched the boy's genitals. He was horrified and hoped the youngster had not taken any notice. However the kid shared it with his father, who confronted Gareth. He was understanding and suggested Gareth had counselling. This he did through the pastor at church and Jane also became aware of the situation. It was a painful time for them both, but ultimately strengthened the marriage. There were no other incidents and the matter was kept confidential.

A month ago Gareth and Jane were talking to their pastor on another matter and he asked if they felt Sandy and her husband, Simon, ought to know about the incident with this young lad. His reasoning was to protect Gareth and Sandy's son. Gareth reacted strongly to this, saying he could not imagine ever telling any of his children. He said he honestly did not think it would be a problem. However, he was shocked to find one of his old sexual fantasies recurring. He became very depressed and Sandy, who is close to her dad, wanted to know what was troubling him. Gareth broke down and said he just could not tell her. Eventually Gareth's depression and the tension in the family persuaded Gareth and Jane to talk about what was going on. It came to a point where they felt nothing could be worse than the tension and fear they were experiencing.

A family conference was organised and Gareth, helped by Jane, talked to his children about his own childhood, sexuality and the incident of ten years ago. Understandably, his daughters and son found it more difficult to handle than their spouses. There was some silence, some anger, but a lot of love and tears. Gareth and Jane had decided the best way to talk about the truth was to unwrap as much of it as possible, rather than sharing one or two feelings which could then be misinterpreted. They encouraged the rest of the family to say how they were feeling and any thoughts which arose, not just at that time, but subsequently.

When the question of Gareth's feelings towards his grandchildren was brought up, everyone agreed that Gareth and Jane should try to feel as natural and unself-conscious as possible with Andrew and any other grand-children. Gareth assured his children that he had never experienced any sexual feelings towards any of them. Sandy admitted that at first she found it difficult when Gareth held her son, Andrew, or cuddled him, but she had worked through this.

Jennifer was frequently sexually abused by her mother between the ages of four and ten. Her mother and father were successful in business and as far as Jennifer is aware, her two younger sisters were not sexually abused. Jennifer's father died when she was twelve, but her mother is still alive. Jennifer has not talked about the sexual abuse with any other family members. She has been receiving counsel-ling for many years. Now in her late thirties and unmarried, she was very promiscuous heterosexually until ten years ago when she became a committed Christian. She has found it difficult to maintain long-term relationships, especially with women.

Jennifer recently confronted her mother with much of what she had done to her. She also explained the long-term effects on herself of the sexual abuse as she understood them. She wanted to be reconciled to her mother, but did not feel this could be achieved until her mother was prepared to accept responsibility for what she had done and asked her daughter's forgiveness. Her mother stated bluntly that she did not consider what had happened to be either wrong or harmful. She told Jennifer she had been a willing party and was now trying to make it an excuse for her own hang-ups. Jennifer refused to accept this and told her mother she would not have any communication with her until she was prepared to accept the wrong she had done. Jennifer has not seen her mother or contacted her since, or received anything from her mother apart from a birthday card and a cheque for twenty pounds which she gave to the NSPCC.

Alice and Joe had been married thirty years. Although much of their social life involved them as a married couple, they had their own friends. Joe was often with his own mates in the pub and Alice accepted this, although she hardly met any of them. There was one younger man whom Joe saw a lot and Alice sometimes felt uneasy about this. She was completely unprepared for Joe's declaration that he was gay and in love with his young friend, Karl. They had been in a gay relationship for the last two years and 'could not live without each other'. Joe was hoping Alice would accept this. He wanted them to live as man and wife for the sake of their teenage children, but Karl would still be his sexual partner. He explained he had no sexual feelings at all for Alice, but still enjoyed her company and their mutual interests. He was surprised at the extent of Alice's hurt and feelings of rejection. They agreed to continue living together. It took Alice a long time to adjust to Karl and Joe's relationship, but eventually they all seemed to be reasonably good friends. The initial feelings of rejection and self-hate which Alice had felt, seemed gradually to become less of an issue for her. Then, Karl and Joe split up. Alice felt a lot more insecure, depressed and anxious about the future. She assumed Joe would find a replacement for Karl. Alice and Joe were divorced in their mid-fifties.

Stephen is thirty and became a Christian ten years ago. He is convinced that homosexual relationships are not compatible with his Christian faith. He has at times found it difficult to follow this ideal, but is very much aware of God's love for him and can testify to real experiences of change and healing in many areas of his life. His parents are not Christians and find it difficult to understand why Stephen should not find a homosexual partner and settle down. His brother has done this and seems quite happy. In fact he seems much more 'normal' than Stephen, in his parents' eyes.

Your Story?

These situations are all very different. Some are far more resolved than others. You may be able to identify with some of the feelings and relationships.

My Story

My own family were aware of my homosexuality and some of my homosexual relationships, but we never talked about it. My brother, Ralph, on the other hand was very open about his homosexuality, with my mother especially. He had a lot of complex personality problems and his homosexual relationships certainly reflected this. Ralph's lifestyle caused my mother and father a lot of pain. I tried to show them through my own life and relationships that I was not like Ralph. Although we never spelt it out to each other, I am sure they knew perfectly well that most of my friends, whom they liked very much, were gay.

When I became a Christian, I began to believe it was wrong to be involved sexually in homosexual relationships and struggled to know how to tell my gay friends. We had always been close and supported each other. In fact, if it had not been for my Christian beliefs I would have been quite happy to continue my homosexual relationships. When I first became a Christian, it was not difficult for me to be celibate. And for this reason I felt I could be quite open with other Christians about my homosexual past. This was all very new to me. I had previously only been open about my sexuality with other gay men. I was encouraged by what seemed to be a very positive response to my openness from other Christians. A few years later I did struggle with homosexual feelings and temptations, but by this time my faith was meaningful enough to prevent me from abandoning Christianity and becoming involved in homosexual relationships again. I have experienced many of the feelings and emotions of people like Pat and Richard (Mark's mother and father), Delroy, Carol and many others. Sometimes it is because of my own experiences and with those I love, but also through the many people who have contacted TfT – a counselling and teaching ministry I helped create and for whom I now work.

Although every situation is different because every person is unique, there are common threads and principles. We will look at some of these and responses to them. We all make moral choices, whether we have a religious faith or not. We all make mistakes in the way we relate to each other, but if we are prepared to work at them, they can be a catalyst to our own growth and healing.

2

Threads of Hope
and Understanding

A tremendous sense of loss is often one of the most tangible experiences when homosexuality is disclosed by a close friend or relative. A sense of loss similar to that of bereavement can be experienced whenever unknown information about someone close to us is revealed. However, it may be even more traumatic when it involves sexuality. As I will emphasise, sexuality is one of the greatest human drives. It involves a lot more than just sexual feelings and experiences. Our basic human need for love and affirmation is the driving force of sexual desire. These strong emotions contribute to a sense of identity and self-acceptance or the lack of it. Modern society seems to encourage this.

Revelations about another person's sexuality and sexual behaviour have the potential to bring some of our strongest human emotions to the surface. We may feel threatened, seeing the revelations as a reflection on us, even when we know in truth they are probably not. These reactions should be accepted as perfectly normal. They are not in themselves judgments. They may soon lead to judgments, often irrational, but this second stage must not be assumed.

Shock

When a close friend or relative tells us some information about themselves which is totally new, we can often feel completely stunned. An icy wind chills or maybe even freezes our very soul. A close relationship involves sharing oneself with another. It means letting the other person know who I really am. Sometimes this will be consciously done by the people involved, deliberately sharing information and listening to the response. Otherwise it will be a natural part of loving and living alongside another person. It is being involved in the very creation of someone's personality.

This is especially true in the case of parents who try to be there for their child at every point in life. The child has been completely dependent on the parent, who is an emotional and practical lifeline supporting the existence of another human being. This sense of knowing another person is much deeper than simply having information and trying to understand it. We each become a part of one another's sense of identity and security. I believe it is primarily this sense of identity with another person that feels so hurt and even vandalised when previously unknown and significant personal information is disclosed.

Shock and even withdrawal does not necessarily mean a rejection of the person. It may be a self-protecting mechanism or an attempt to flee from the pain.

Anger

The same can be true of anger. It will usually be irrational. It can be compared with the anger sometimes experienced after the death of a loved one. The anger then may be addressed at the other person for dying: 'How could you die and leave me like this!' Anger needs to be expressed safely, rather than buried. Feeling angry is, however, an expression of love – one of the many paradoxes in human emotions. I can be angry with someone for dying and yet it is not usually the other person's fault. This is a good example to use because so many people say that when previously unknown information about someone's sexuality was disclosed, it seemed as if they had died. 'The person I thought I knew has gone. This person seems like a stranger to me!' I am conscious that this response can sound judgmental. It seems as if I am saying I do not like what I am hearing and therefore do not approve. This may ultimately be the response, but not necessarily at this stage. It is primarily that someone with whom I felt close now seems like a stranger. This is devastating. Just as after a loss through death, life will never be the same again.

A Long Process

It will probably take a long time to work through this form of bereavement. The length of time needed will depend on the situation and the feelings of all involved. For example, Wendy and David, Gary's mother and father, seemed to work through it very quickly. They were not apparently unhappy about Gary's homosexual lifestyle. Following the initial shock the new identity did not seem particularly to trouble them. Sometimes this reaction will come from a deep-rooted moral conviction, at other times from a desire to keep everyone happy. In the case of Rachel and Delroy the bereavement process is likely to take a long time. Delroy not only has to cope with an apparent loss of the identity of the person he loved, but also with a wife.

Bereavement through marital or relationship breakdown usually takes longer to work through than bereavement through the death of a partner. Some would say that there is always some pain left.

Bargaining

Delroy may also be sensing a loss of his perception of his masculinity and even his own sexuality. His mind may start to fill with thoughts of: 'If only . . .' 'If only I had been more attractive.' 'If only I had loved her differently.' 'If only I had pleased her more sexually.' Inevitably, one of the first questions asked by a person to whom a disclosure of homosexuality has been made is: 'Where did I go wrong?'

Living in Denial

Rachel may also be feeling torn emotionally. She may try to cope with this by denying to herself what is really happening. She appears to have no regard for or appreciation of Delroy's feelings or even their children's. Facing up to the full implications of the situation is too painful and threatens to cause an overwhelming sense of guilt. This type of living in denial does not always last for a long time, but in some cases it does. Denying the truth of my feelings and those of others involved becomes a part of my everyday 'sense of being'. This is almost certainly the case with Jennifer's mum. She resolutely refuses to take responsibility for the abuse of Jennifer. It may be that her conscience really is convinced she has done nothing wrong. More likely, she has sought to convince herself in order to avoid the pain of guilt. She is not only denying herself reconciliation with Jennifer and forgiveness from God, but also undermining her own self-worth. Part of being human lies in being given responsibility. Opting out by refusing to admit a wrongdoing is in a way rejecting personal value or self-worth.

It is so important to recognise that all these feelings are perfectly normal ways (not always appropriate) in which human nature responds to extraordinary situations. They should not be assumed to be an accurate picture of the way things were or the way they are now.

An initial response to the situation, therefore, should be accepted as simply that. Conclusions about the future of the relationship should not be made during this initial response, either by the person sharing the information or the person on the receiving end. I hope this book will cover both perspectives. We need to accept how people may respond if we disclose our own homosexuality, as well as anticipating some reactions in ourselves when someone tells us about their homosexuality. We will need to give ourselves time and space to grieve and adjust or give others their own time and space to work through these initial responses.

Unwrapping the Gift

Acceptance is likely to take time. Some will be more able to receive the new information and accept it than others. It might be helpful to see it as unwrapping a gift. It may or may not be something we want. It has been given to us and it may have cost the other person a lot in terms of risking rejection and misunderstanding. As we start to unwrap the gift, the contents reveal themselves. We may not get far in the process before we find we have to stop. We cannot

receive any more for the moment. That is fine. We may
need to examine more closely what we have already dis-
covered before we go on to anything else. The person who
has given the gift also needs to allow the other time to
unwrap it.

The acceptance process is very important in itself. It does not
mean approval or disapproval in the long term. We must be
aware of making sweeping judgments about the gift of self-
disclosure, whether we are the giver or the receiver of the
gift.

Filters and Messages

The information we receive is filtered through our own
feelings and our image of self and others. This has developed as a result of every relationship and experience in our
lives, right from the moment of conception. Messages have
been received about ourselves and others through the way
we have been loved or unloved. Some messages have been
truthfully received by us, others have been misinterpreted,
often as a result of circumstances beyond anyone's control.

For example, our parents may have high expectations for
us. They may want us to achieve and experience all the
things in life they could not experience themselves. They
may want our lives to be exactly like theirs, again believing
this is the best for us. The message we are being given is:
'We want the very best for you because we think you are
worth it.' This message is very positive and may be received
as such. On the other hand it may not. I may actually
believe that certain standards and behaviour patterns are
being demanded of me and that my value and acceptance is
dependent on them. If this is so, the message I may be
receiving is: 'You will only be acceptable to me if you

conform to the image I have for you. You must be what I want you to be!' This is not necessarily the message intended, but it is what we have received. Sometimes the message received was indeed given.

Mark's father, Richard, finds it difficult to express feelings. The message he received as a child was: 'Men should not cry.' He appreciated this and although he learned to feel safe to express emotions, it often frustrated him. Mark's disclosure of his homosexuality challenged Richard's perception of himself and eventually he allowed himself to cry. Likewise, we may be aware of misconceptions we have carried from childhood and try to react very differently with our own children. On the other hand we may have certain expectations for them. In a way, it is perfectly all right to have expectations – to want what we perceive to be the very best for another person. However, it is important that we balance this with a sense of acceptance that actually says: 'I love and accept you as you are. You don't have to be different in order to be loved by me.'

Close relationships involve being a part of another's life and therefore being involved in the shaping and moulding of another, just as that person is involved in our own growth process. This is true in all very close relationships and especially in parenthood. If our loved one shares something about him- or herself that is such a fundamental part of their personality as sexuality, then I will not only be affected by that, but may actually see it as a reflection on me.

When I was in college, many fellow students knew about my homosexual background. We often used to meet in pairs to talk and pray together. Many confessed they felt threatened by me. This was not because they feared I would seduce them or would become romantically involved. It was rather that they feared I would see something in them they would rather not know about. They were not necessarily struggling to deny homosexual feelings, it was just that something had happened in their life that made them, at times, question their own sexuality. For example, they may have been involved in homosexuality at school. Some had experienced the close attachment of a homosexual friend who hoped the feelings would be returned. This led the person to wonder if they were giving off homosexual vibes of which they were unaware.

One person recognised such feelings in himself and was determined he would work through them by getting to know me as a person. This was not at all patronising. He simply wanted to discover the real me, while dealing with what he recognised as his own fears and prejudices. As this began to happen, he says, he stopped seeing me as a homosexual, but rather as a person, warts and all. We have been close friends ever since.

The process of acceptance, therefore, involves identifying the complex feelings within ourselves, and recognising they are there because of our own experiences and the messages we have received about ourselves and other people. The images that we have of ourselves, as well as the image that we have of homosexuality, will be to some extent distorted. This is why it is so important that we do not allow initial responses, whatever they may be, negative or positive, to determine the future of our relationship with a loved one. This must also be true for the person who has shared. It will be easier to accept the truth when we know ourselves well enough to identify what is filtering it.

Acceptance is seeking to identify the truth of the situation and my feelings as well as those of my loved one: 'This is the way it is.'

The Gift of Self-Disclosure

Many people who disclose their homosexuality do so as an act of love. For some it may be one of the most costly ways they have ever expressed love for someone else. It is risking rejection, seeking to overcome fear and wanting another person to share in a very important part of their humanity. If it is apparently rejected, that can be devastating. A sense of trust and security may feel violated. It is crucial for both people in the sharing process to appreciate this.

If the reason you want to disclose your homosexuality is because of your love for your parents or close friends, it is important you tell them this. Rather than simply announcing you are homosexual and revealing it like a label or badge you have been hiding, it should be shared as a part of the 'real you'. This means you talk about the way you feel about the whole situation, including your fears. That may sound like emotional blackmail, but it is helping someone to see more of the whole picture rather than simply the label you may believe describes it. Labels do not usually tell us much and can easily be misinterpreted. John Powell in his book *Why Am I Afraid to Tell You Who I Am?* says: 'The greatest gift of love is self-disclosure.' If someone is taking that kind of costly risk with us, then we are privileged.

I am contacted by many Christians who say to me: 'I have never shared this with anyone else before!' This puts me and people like me in a tremendously privileged position, even though it is a sad reflection on the quality of love in the church. Sometimes the shock and hurt felt in the person receiving this gift of love can make it seem unappreciated. However, once the dust has settled, its true value may be seen. Appreciation can certainly be communicated even if the hurt, fear and anger are also being felt. None of this negates the gift of self-disclosure.

I often find in my own relationships and those of close friends who share about their sexuality, the response is to reciprocate with another gift of sharing. I have known this happen in close friendships and the parent–child relationship. The gift of self-disclosure and the cost involved is so much appreciated, that the person longs to respond with another gift. This mutual act of costly love might be experienced right at the beginning of the acceptance process, or it may come at a later stage. However, it is important for these basic qualities of costly love to be understood and appreciated. The 'gift of self-disclosure' should be given, rather than just the label or the wrapping. This may be done in stages, with the other's permission.

Gifts to Get Even

There will be times when the revelation of a loved one's homosexuality is not intended as a gift, but rather ammunition to deliberately hurt and perhaps punish. The loved one feels hurt and offended, using the declaration of homosexuality as retribution to hurt and offend in response. It is said that love and hate are often closely associated.

Judith's husband Michael had a father from a very strict Christian background who often spoke out very loudly against homosexuality. Michael felt hurt and rejected by his father, and this came to the surface in a row when Michael's dad had been harshly condemning homosexuals in a play on TV. Michael felt even more hurt and rejected by his father, responding by telling him about his own homosexuality in a violent outburst. His father was initially stunned into silence and then wept uncontrollably. He does not speak out against homosexuals any more.

Sadly, there are times when the initial response is not one of seeking to accept or understand, but outright rejection. The relationship seems utterly destroyed. However, reconciliation may be possible even if there seems a complete breakdown.

Accepting the Gift

The gift! How can I possibly even think of what I'm going through as a gift? The word implies something good – something I want to receive. This is why it can seem an unfortunate word to choose in these situations. I use it because I find it a helpful way of learning to accept people and circumstances. The gift is not necessarily what we want or feel we need. It might be an unpleasant thing, so please do not think I'm trying to underestimate, trivialise or be triumphalistic about personal trauma and pain.

Perhaps the first stage is to acknowledge the nature of the gift as we perceive it. It may well be something we do not want. It may be painful and difficult to handle. It may be something that we do not want to look at, let alone unwrap. Nevertheless, it cannot go away and we will not be able to move forward in any healthy way in our own lives, until we have looked at the gift and begun to unwrap it. This will take time because the gift is fragile and so are we! The process of acceptance involves unwrapping the gift and identifying it, both in terms of its wrapping and contents. As I have said, the feelings of the person unwrapping the gift will affect the way it is seen. In a way the receiver's feelings and reactions are a reciprocal gift. Both people are receiving gifts from each other, which involve feelings and information. As we unwrap each other's gifts of self-disclosure, we become more able to see and hopefully understand one another.

Communication and Listening

How do we do this? The answer must lie in the way that we communicate. Communication means allowing the other person to talk, and listening to what they are saying. Like everything else in the unwrapping process, our own feelings, hurts and insecurities are likely to cause us to misunderstand and misinterpret what the other is saying. This may not be true, but we need to be aware it is a possibility. One way to avoid this is to feed back to the other person what we believe has been said and listen to their response.

This kind of communication can sound easy in theory, but it is not so easy in practice. I often find myself so full of nervous tension in these situations that to communicate what I am feeling can be difficult. It all seems to sound wrong. It is made so much easier when the person receiving the gift of my self-disclosure helps and encourages me to share, by gently unwrapping it with me. I believe the ground rule must be honesty and a willingness to share how we are feeling at each stage of the process. Listening to the other is absolutely crucial. So often, we can be so worried and confused by what we are hearing, thinking we have to offer some kind of response or answer, when we should be more concerned to receive the information and understand what is being said.

Listening in this way can be especially difficult for parents. Our child has been for so long our responsibility that we feel we must always be available to help and provide answers for all life's problems. We know in theory that once a child has matured they need to become their own person and make their own decisions, but it can sometimes be difficult to give them this freedom. That in itself may be a bereavement process we have been through or have yet to experience. We may be relating to our loved one as if we are the parent (that is, the protector or rescuer).

Acceptance Is Not Agreement

Acceptance is a process of knowing as much as possible about the situation and the feelings involved. It does not necessarily mean a complete understanding or condoning. Acceptance by the person with homosexual feelings and the relative or friend with whom it is shared, is important if both are going to move on in their own growth process. Mutual honesty should enable me to identify and accept my own feelings in either role in this situation.

As a friend or relative of the homosexual person, my own morality and possibly theology will affect the way I accept what is being shared. However, at this initial stage of the process it can be a good idea to put it to one side. I do not mean one should give the impression one is happy with what is going on, when this is not true, but the priority at this stage is to accept and receive the information being given. The moral choices and responses we all have to make, can only be made effectively when we have done this. As a Christian I believe that God, my Creator, is the only one who fully understands all about me and my loved ones. I find the truth of this a tremendous source of security and comfort, even though my understanding will always be limited.

When I was in my late teens I never talked to my parents about my homosexuality and homosexual relationships. One reason was to prevent undue worry and anxiety. My brother was also homosexual and often attracted to men from a fairly deprived social environment. He enjoyed entertaining and impressing them, lavishly. My parents and I saw ourselves as 'respectable' middle-class people, and the fairly rough and scruffy men my brother used to occasionally bring home caused my parents considerable anxiety. That was a long time ago and I hope the same reaction would not be there today.

I overheard my brother telling my parents about my homosexuality, so I knew they were aware of what was going on, but I still did not talk to them about it and they did not mention it. Once I assumed they knew, I went to a lot of trouble trying to convince them my friends were 'nice and respectable'. I thought they probably realised we were all gay. I was trying to tell them something, but holding an awful lot back. It was a subtle, not very honest form of communication. I regret this. It caused a barrier between myself and my parents which was never completely broken down. Once the secrecy and lack of real communication was set in place, it became difficult to break through that. I could not see the point in doing so at the time.

My mother died a couple of years after I became a Christian. Two years later the ministry in which I am now involved began. My father was living with me and so had to know about my homosexual background and my Christianity. That was good in lots of ways, but I still found it very difficult indeed to communicate my feelings to him. Because I had not shared anything of my feelings as a gay man with my parents, I also found it difficult to share my feelings as a Christian man. I find many parents come to see me when their child, as an adult, has disclosed their homosexuality. I often feel that at least it must be good that the person has shared something. It has to be a good start.

The Gift of Responsibility

I believe that God created us with a free will. We all have the freedom to do good things or bad things, helpful or unhelpful. It is an important part of our value as human beings, the value which comes from being given responsibility. This gift is often betrayed and abused. The value of the person who abuses his or her own responsibility as well as that of another person is diminished. For example, children from a family where one or both parents has a significant personality problem (for example, alcoholism) often feel they have to take some responsibility for their parent. This is both an abuse of the parent's sense of responsibility and also an abuse of the child, who should not be responsible for the parent. This sense of being responsible for another can, in varying degrees, affect the adult who then feels a need to be responsible for others in ways which are not healthy. The value of both persons is undermined.

Parents or parent role models have to take some responsibility for their children who are totally dependent on them initially. It can be difficult to balance the right sense of responsibility, with the need to let the child be their own person and giving them the gift of their own responsibility. When the parent or parent role model has responsibility for the child, it can be difficult to let go of that when they become an adult. It can seem like changing a whole mode of behaviour and feelings. Even the sense of identity of the parent can seem to be lost. It can feel as if a

major source of purpose and value in life has gone. The
process of letting go is much more difficult for some than
for others. But in my opinion it is vital the child who is
now adult is given their gift of responsibility. There has to
be a deliberate 'letting go'. This is another gift. It does not
mean an abdication of help and support, but is setting a
person free 'to be'. This is true in the parent-to-child and
child-to-parent relationship, but also in other friendships
and relationships. Perhaps it is a reflection of the way in
which God, our Creator, has given us a free will to accept
or reject him – to believe or disbelieve.

This means that in the communication process of listening, understanding and accepting, both the person disclos-
ing homosexuality and the person receiving this disclosure,
need to give each other the gift of personal responsibility.
In my own relationship as a young man with my mother
and father, I was not prepared to do this. I was trying to
protect them from being hurt, but in the process building a
barrier of secrecy in our own relationships. I was not giving
them the gift of their own responsibility, allowing them to
respond in their way to my own situation. Perhaps I was
also denying myself some responsibility by seeking to hide
the truth from them. If only I had given them the truth of
how I was feeling, which also meant sharing my fears of
worrying them, our relationships could have been very
different. The same applies from their side, but I can't take
responsibility for that! Perhaps we were alike.

The process of letting go is such an important way of
communicating love and acceptance on both sides. It does
not mean that having 'let go', you no longer communicate
with each other, unless this is your choice. It does help to
clear away material which obstructs communication and
understanding. The process will probably be worked

through much more speedily as each person learns to let go of the other and communicates this by listening and seeking to understand, rather than struggling to respond with answers, solutions or rescue packages.

The Gift of Prayer

Letting go often leaves a sense of utter helplessness and this is where I find prayer helps. In communicating how I am feeling to God (the only one who fully understands) and praying for my loved one, I know I am doing something to help, without taking away the other person's responsibility or abdicating my own.

Sometimes, continually bringing a situation before God can encourage my mind to think about it so much that it becomes more difficult to let go. A trusted friend can be helpful in this situation. Another who shares the burden in prayer can take some pressure and sense of responsibility from me. There must be clear ground rules. The person must be trustworthy and pledged to confidentiality. He or she must also be willing to let go and not interfere. Perhaps even more importantly, the person I am praying for should give permission for the situation to be disclosed with someone else. If this is too threatening for our loved one and it may well be, we can simply ask a close friend to pray, without specifying a problem or sharing a confidence.

Pat and Richard, the Christian parents of a homosexual son, Mark, were able to ask a few close friends to pray for their son. A couple of friends knew about the situation; Mark had asked his parents to tell them. However, nothing more than Mark's homosexuality and his relationship were shared. The prayers offered continually were that everyone involved in the situation would know and receive the love

of Christ. This apparently simple prayer still reaches the
heart of God who knows and understands more about the
situation and the feelings of everyone involved than anyone
else.

I often picture the person or people for whom I am
praying, in my mind, and in this way bring them before the
Lord. Symbolically, it also helps me to let go and give them
to God.

Many people testify to answered prayer of this sort. The
love of Christ often breaks dramatically into a person's
situation, even when the pray-er knows nothing about it. I
will never forget praying for a loved one who had run away
from home in a desperate mental state. I received a
message, saying he was in the casualty department of a local
hospital. I simply prayed, I felt very inadequately, that he
would know the love of Jesus. My friend later told me he
was semiconscious when he arrived, alone, at the hospital.
The doctor in casualty held his hand and having asked his
name whispered, 'Jesus loves you, James.' Some time later
a young doctor was speaking at my church. He mentioned
in passing that he worked in the casualty department of our
local hospital. I had not met this person before, but ended
up talking with him, after the service. He was the doctor
concerned. Apparently, my friend was very distressed and
the young doctor felt God wanted him to express his love
to James. He had no idea, before meeting me, that his
patient was a Christian.

I had felt my prayer lacked faith and meaning. I was
wrong. It must have meant something to James, and the
reminder of the incident also encouraged the doctor a
couple of years later. The apostle Paul describes the depths
of prayer: '*We do not know what we ought to pray, but the
Spirit himself intercedes for us with groans that words cannot*

express' (*Rom. 8:26*). What an amazing mystery, that God himself through the Holy Spirit prays for us! He is the greatest of all prayer warriors.

The Ministry of Listening

As a Christian, the question I should always ask is: 'How would God respond in this situation?' There is not often an easy answer, but I must work at it. God is the perfect listener who lets us hear ourselves as we share everything with him. I have mentioned the filters created by our life experiences – some truth, some lies – received by us. God the Creator is the only one without a filter. He receives all our information and emotions without any fear and prejudice.

Humanly speaking, I will never fully understand God. His nature is so very different from mine. There appear to be mysteries and paradoxes. He hates sin and suffering, but allows it. He longs for us to follow and obey him. He grieves when we reject his love, but has given us the freedom to do that.

We can never listen as perfectly as God, but we can work at it.

3

How Does It All Begin?

Nature or Nurture?

There are so many theories about how homosexuality is caused. New research which seems to show there is a 'gay gene' is often greeted with joy. At last, it is argued, we can say homosexuality is as natural and normal as left-handedness! Is there a 'gay gene'? I don't know. I do not believe something as variable and complex as a person's sexuality can possibly be traced back to a single gene. There could be a genetic component that affects the way I react to situations and relationships, but a sexual feeling of any type has not simply been born within me. After all, we don't seem to argue for genetic causes of other types of sexual feelings and desires. Why just simply homosexual ones? Sexual desires are so different for each person.

Reasons for Debate – Fear and Prejudice

One problem, as I see it, is that many people hope homosexuality will be proved to be genetic in origin so that homosexuals can be more acceptable in society. The hope is that this will encourage less fear and prejudice. I believe fear and prejudice are absolutely alien to the Spirit of God, who says, *'There is no fear in love'* (*1 John 4:18*), but I am not convinced that proving there is a gay gene will stop homophobia (fear of homosexuality).

Sexuality is far more than the sexual desire I may have for another person. It also influences the way I feel about myself and what I believe others may think about me.

I do quite a lot of public speaking on this subject. I hate confrontation and often wonder if some members of the audience will bombard me with irrational hatred of homosexual people. I often make the observation that people who shout the loudest against homosexuality are often those who secretly struggle with homosexual feelings themselves. I don't usually hear a murmur! This is certainly true when I know my listeners are Christians who believe that homosexual acts are not compatible with Christianity.

It is less easy to avoid confrontation when addressing those who believe my Christian moral choices are anti-homosexual. What does this prove? Perhaps that we are all likely to be expressing some fear and prejudice when relating to someone else's sexuality. The militant gay activist and the fundamentalist Christian may both be expressing fear and prejudice in different ways.

Admitting Fear

As a parent, relative or friend of a person with homosexual feelings, or as that person, it is important to recognise our fears and prejudices. Our reaction to the issue, whatever that may be, is an expression of our own sexuality. When looking at how a person's sexuality may develop, I am conscious of the range of emotions you, the reader, may have in response to what I am saying. This is especially true of parents, who may already be experiencing self-recrimination, probably unjustified. It is more than likely that you would not feel as anxious or guilty if your child had feelings like jealousy, self-centredness, insecurity or loneliness. Sexuality somehow seems very different from emotional problems, but in reality it is not. As I said before, what makes it seem different is the influence of our own sexuality. This is an expression of fear. As mentioned earlier, fear is not loving. Therefore the fear of another's sexuality or of my own is not an expression of godly love – no matter how natural and understandable it may seem.

Guilt

A natural part of the grieving process which I have tried to describe, is often guilt, which may be irrational. In looking at how we may become homosexual, I do not want to be misunderstood and feed any problem of guilt. The often strong reactions against homosexual people can, for many parents, increase the burdens of guilt and helplessness. However, as with many homosexuals themselves, some parents respond by affirming homosexuality. Gary's parents supported their son and were saying, 'Gary's homosexuality is good and not something for which any of us should feel guilt or shame.' Mark's parents, Pat and Richard, were initially carrying much more guilt and self-condemnation, which would ultimately become transformed by God.

Truth

Stepping into what can seem like a minefield of feelings will be much easier if we can lay some foundations of truth. Our reactions and responses may make true perspectives difficult to see. We cannot be fully objective. I believe strongly that, although feelings are important, it is ultimately the truth which sets us free from self-recrimination. We will look more at how that can be experienced.

Try to take away the 'homosexual label'. That is not at all easy in a society which likes to give everything a name and identity, to make us feel more secure. The label may even give us something to conform to.

Sexuality is not simply sex. It involves emotions driven by love – sometimes very apparent, sometimes not. Even self-gratifying sex, like masturbation, has – its driving force – a desire to be loved.

Emotions and sexuality cannot be separated. They are complexly interlinked. We were not born with our emotional make-up, neatly intact.

Messages

The way we feel about ourselves and others has resulted from a multitude of influences – some good, some bad – we have received from other people, circumstances and possibly our genes. Some of these 'messages' have been intended for us; many others have been misinterpretations. In other words, the messages we have received and believed have often, in truth, not been those intended by the givers. We do not let all these experiences wash over our heads. We respond to them. We may even make internal statements (a life's motto, perhaps) – 'I am not acceptable' or 'My value depends on what I do for others.' They may be vows, such as, 'I will not let anyone get close to me' or 'I must be totally vulnerable with everyone.'

Some of these responses become 'sexualised'. That is to say, some of these responses become sexual feelings.

No one has had a life free from distorted messages. It is a part of everyday life and relationships. It is so important to recognise this. No one has a perfect image of self and others.

Our distorted images are usually reflected in our relationships. Sometimes we will be aware of this and consciously seek to act accordingly, in what we believe is the right way, but often we may be totally unaware of what we are carrying with us into our relationships. Homosexuality is just one possible response to experiences and feelings.

Homosexuality has not necessarily developed as a result of parental problems or mistreatment. The vast majority of homosexuals and lesbians have come from homes which most of us would regard as perfectly healthy and 'normal'.

Unmet Needs

Dr Elizabeth Moberly, in her book *Homosexuality: A New Christian Ethic* (James Clarke), says homosexuality is the 'result of a legitimate same sex need from childhood, which has to some extent remained unmet'. This same-sex need, as I understand it, is a vital factor in the development of self-worth, value and identity (a sense of 'being'). This childhood need is to receive positive messages about oneself from a significant same-sex role model very early in life.

However, in my experience, this process is incredibly fragile and as I said before, is affected by other factors than simply the significant same-sex relationship itself. Experiences quite outside anyone's control can contribute to this emotional deficit – a difficult birth, absent parent or role model through illness or even possibly genetic factors.

As a response to this deficit the child will tend to withdraw, to some extent, from this early same-sex relationship, and make a vow, 'I will not allow you to get close to me.' This can mean that no matter how much the parent or role model tries to affirm the child, the same-sex adult is actually rejected by the child.

With so many factors involved in our emotional and sexual development, none of us is totally unaffected, no matter how good we may believe our parents have been. Conversely, not everyone who has experienced something of these emotional deficits experiences homosexual feelings.

Change

None of us is completely without any emotional deficits in our upbringing; no one can say for sure that these same-sex needs will not surface in a sexual way.

I meet many people who have been unaware of homosexual feelings and apparently totally heterosexual, often very actively so. Then in a particularly close same-sex friendship they experience homosexual and emotional feelings for the first time. The relationship has brought to the surface some previously unrecognised unmet same-sex needs, which have become sexualised. This does not mean that all close emotional bonding between members of the same sex will become sexual. The discovery of previously unexperienced sexual feelings can also happen for the homosexual and lesbian. Sometimes, as the same-sex needs are met, relationships with the opposite sex become more meaningful emotionally and heterosexual feelings surface. This does not usually mean that there will never be any more homosexual desires. I have met many Christians who experience this as they work with God and other Christians at the underlying issues involved in the development of their homosexuality. They are therefore sometimes able to get married.

Marriage Not the Answer

Heterosexual marriage must never be seen as the answer to homosexuality. Some people, including many Christians, have entered marriage believing it to be a way of dealing with their loneliness and homosexuality. They have often felt this was God's will for their lives and have been actively encouraged to believe this by other Christians. The results have been tragic and caused much hurt, anger and disillusionment for all involved.

Delroy and Rachel's experiences, told in Chapter 1, are not uncommon. Rachel had thought her lesbianism had gone when she became a Christian. Although she mentioned it to Delroy early on in their relationship, he had not even wondered if it might still be an issue. Sadly, Rachel's spirituality had also encouraged her to deny the feelings that were still there. Now they had returned very powerfully in Rachel's relationship with Ella. She no longer wanted to deny these strong desires. At last, she felt, 'I am going to be true to myself.' We will be looking at some of these very important spiritual issues in a later chapter.

Pat and Richard loved their only son, Mark. They saw him as an answer to their prayers. Richard had always found it difficult to express his feelings. His own father's army career and strict schooling certainly had a lot to do with this. 'Boys aren't allowed to cry' 'stiff upper lip' were very much part of the ethos which influenced him. Once he had become a committed Christian, in his late teens, Richard appreciated what a mistake the freeze on his emotions had been. However, no matter how hard he tried, his emotions only defrosted very slowly. Fifteen years after Mark was born, Richard had a wonderful experience of God's love and power. This resulted in a tremendous release of his frozen emotions.

When Mark was a child, Richard was a devoted parent. He tried to make sure that his son would not have the strict regime he had as a child. He was very successful in business and often travelled abroad. One of Richard's motivations in working so hard was to give his son the very best of everything. He especially longed for Mark to have more academic qualifications than he was able to achieve. He often said this was not the most important thing in life, but this message was not fully received by Mark. The message Mark was given by his father was, 'You mean so much to me that I will do anything for you.' However, because of many factors, the message Mark received as a very young child was different. It was something like: 'You are not so special. However, you might be if you become more academic.' Tragically, Mark's misinterpretation of his father's love was the complete opposite of the truth. Tony, Mark's lover, is very academic.

Consequent Attractions

Mark seems to be attracted to the person he 'feels' he would like to be in order to be acceptable. This is the way he responded to those negative yet untrue messages he received. Other homosexual people may respond differently. Some people with Mark's background will be attracted to someone completely non-academic. Usually homosexual attraction is to the person 'I would like to be' or the person 'I would like to have been'. People from a similar background to Mark's will not necessarily develop homosexual feelings.

Gareth (the married man attracted to boys) is to some extent seeking to experience his childhood once again. Perhaps a fear of responsibility or another aspect of adulthood is threatening and childhood seems more attractive and safer? I have met a few men and women sexually attracted to children. In nearly every case the desire is to be loved and accepted by the child. This can sometimes be expressed by desiring to please the child sexually. Even in apparently strong, mature men and women, childlike vulnerability and innocence can sometimes be seen. Tragically, when expressed sexually, it can have devastating consequences in the young life it abuses.

It is sometimes assumed that sexual abusers of children are always men. Although this issue is more common in men, some women do have sexual feelings for children. In Jennifer's life the abuse from her mother has grossly distorted her image of herself and other women. This seems to have resulted in heterosexual activity, but homosexual feelings could surface at some time, possibly even expecting to be abused again. Sadly, one of the messages received as a result of abuse is that the victim is worth abusing.

The process of emotional and sexuality development is different for each person, with so many factors involved. It is incredibly complex and as unique as a fingerprint.

Parental Responses

Gary's parents, David and Wendy, seem happily to accept his homosexuality. They do not seem to feel any more responsible for it than other personality traits. It was not always like that. At first they went through a fairly natural process of blaming themselves. That is a natural part of their feeling a sense of responsibility as his parents. Perhaps, through meeting Gary's friends, the social stigma of Gary's homosexuality was removed. I believe this in itself is good.

This may sound a strange statement for a Christian to make. However, I believe it is wonderfully true to the gospel or 'good news' of God's love. It is doing what many of us as Christians claim to do, but where we sadly often fail. It is accepting the person and not seeing his or her personhood as any better or worse than anyone else. It is not saying we are happy or unhappy about a lifestyle or behaviour.

Both Gary's parents and Mark's had been able to come to that place in different ways. Any sense of guilt or responsibility for their son's homosexuality had been taken from them. Pat and Richard were able to understand some of the factors involved in Mark's homosexuality, but saw this in the perspective of his uniqueness and value as a person. They were sad Mark was not following Christ, but this would have been just as true if he was a non-Christian heterosexual. Although they regretted some of the factors involved in Mark's upbringing, they realised the same could be true for their own parents and most others. They were grateful that some emotions which had become sexualised in Mark were also expressed in his sensitivity and gentleness. Stephen's non-Christian parents probably found it more difficult to cope with his Christianity than his homosexual orientation.

Not Contagious

A person cannot become homosexual or lesbian through someone else's homosexuality or lesbianism. The potential towards homosexuality – whether it be genetic, emotional, environmental, or a combination of all three – needs to be there in the first place. This can be brought to the surface and expressed with another homosexual, but it can surface in many other same-sex relationships. Its expression can be just as different for each person's situation as heterosexuality.

Michael, the married man with homosexual feelings, had a very close relationship with his son, Adam. Adam was not aware of any homosexual feelings. Perhaps Michael's emotional feelings for the same sex had made Adam less likely to have same-sex emotional deficits. Michael used to worry a lot that he would have sexual feelings for Adam, once Adam had matured and developed sexually. Although he was able to recognise that if Adam had not been his son, he might have found him sexually attractive, there was not a temptation. He wondered if this was partly because he did not want a sexual relationship with his son or through his son's lack of homosexuality. There seems to be no question of Adam responding to Michael sexually, even though he is affectionate with his father. Michael has realised his situation is no different from that faced by many heterosexual fathers with their daughters.

Single Parents

Single parent families are not more likely to have homosexual children than anyone else, because there are so many possible factors involved, rather than simply one relationship. A major issue which sometimes results in homosexuality would seem to be some problem, even a very subtle one, in the communication process. It may have been avoidable or unavoidable. There may have been relationship problems because of emotional deficits, which we all have. On the other hand, something could have happened beyond anyone's control which encouraged a breakdown in communication. The human element may not have been a factor in single parent situations because both parents may have been present in the crucial early years of a child's life. A parental role model may have replaced the missing father or mother. Another reason may be that if there is no possibility of communication, with the absent parent, then there is no breakdown. However, I believe that, ideally, there should be positive relationships with both male and female role models, if natural parents are not around.

Some Family Influences

My father and mother were good parents in many ways. I felt loved by them both and knew they would always be there for me. Having said that, I can remember as a child having nightmares about being orphaned. It may be tempting to read too much into this, but it could have been connected with my mother's fears of a difficult birth when she was pregnant with me. She tended to internalise her anxiety, rather than outwardly expressing it. I may have received something of this, whilst in the womb. That may be hard for some people to take seriously, but our bodies do react to our feelings and tensions. As back sufferers, for example, may know only too well, inner tension and anxiety are often the cause. This is why as a part of its mother's body, the unborn child may receive some of the mother's feelings.

My brother, who was thirteen years older, was a charismatic, somewhat larger-than-life, personality. He was an actor and I wanted to be like him. However, this seemed impossible because I was very shy. My brother's own problems had so much to do with his low self-esteem. As an adult I eventually became aware of this, but a little child is not a psychotherapist. He reacts to what he sees and feels, not to whatever may underlie it. My father's personality was for me overshadowed by my brother's. I guess my brother was my role model, rather than my father.

I can honestly say I do not blame anyone for my homosexuality, nor should I. Perhaps this has not been an issue for me because I have not seen it as a social stigma. My brother encouraged an acceptance of homosexuality and my parents seemed to agree with this, although I think his own sexual behaviour was seen by them as one of his many other problems. They were nevertheless impressed by his intellect. I tried to give the impression that my homosexuality was a much more socially acceptable kind.

Sexual Abuse

Sexual abuse in childhood can also be a factor, in the development of homosexuality, especially of lesbianism. For example, a girl sexually abused by her father will almost certainly grow up with a very distorted image of men and herself. The child may also give some blame to the mother for what happened, even when her mother knew nothing about it. This is because she 'naturally' assumes her mother should protect her, but is equally terrified to seek that protection. The adult victim of childhood sexual abuse by her father may now seek the protection from a mother-figure and this becomes sexual. Child abusers usually threaten their victims, demanding they keep what has happened, or is happening, a secret. The lack of protection the little girl perceives from her mother will cause a deficit in that relationship and this, combined with a negative image of men, can sometimes (not always) be a major root of lesbianism. Another may be the very negative image of oneself that sexual abuse gives the victim. This leads to sexual attraction for the person the abused would like to be.

Women abused by men are often attracted to homosexual men, because they are less threatening sexually and may feel comfortable with a woman's control. Sadly this often results in difficult marriages.

Tim blamed himself for his parents' (Delroy and Rachel) marital breakdown. This was clearly not the case, but is a common reaction in children. It emphasises the need for parents to make every effort in communicating to their children that they are not responsible for the breakdown of a marriage relationship.

Sexual and emotional feelings are responses to messages received, often misinterpreted, about oneself and others.

4

True to the Bible

As I write this book, the issue of homosexuality in the Church is hitting the headlines once again. Some people claim that homosexual relationships are perfectly compatible with Christianity, others say they offend God. You may have deep convictions about this issue. On the other hand, perhaps you have no thoughts on this at all or do not identify yourself as a Bible-believing Christian? I have strong feelings about what I believe the Bible says, and as a Christian I seek to apply biblical principles to every area of my life, including my sexuality. However, in the next chapter I will try to be fair in sharing some of the other viewpoints held, as well as my own.

Honesty

Throughout this book I have tried to encourage an attitude of honesty with oneself in terms of recognising and owning our own feelings. This is also vital as we approach the Bible. Feelings about homosexuality are likely to get in the way of receiving God's truth and of understanding what he is trying to say to us through Scripture. We see this in many different ways. Some of us will want Scripture to tell us homosexual relationships are perfectly acceptable to God, because we want them to be so. There have been times when I have felt this. Or we may feel homosexuality is so distasteful that we will find it difficult to believe God can possibly feel differently about it. We will therefore want the Bible to tell us clearly that homosexual relationships are wrong. It might be helpful for you to pause at this stage, before we go any further, and identify your own feelings.

In the Beginning

The first book of the Bible, Genesis, gives us the context in which to see a biblical perspective of homosexuality. Genesis 2 gives us an account of the creation. Humans (male and female) are created in the image of our Creator, God. The woman was created from the man and they became one flesh together. I will say a bit more about this later. We are told that the man and his wife were naked and felt no shame. This implies there was a sexual purity and innocence we know little of today. Perhaps there was only sexual attraction between the man and his wife. It is possible to read too much into this, but we know at this point in time that the man and his wife had a perfect relationship with God and each other.

The Fall

The man and his wife had been forbidden to eat fruit from the tree in the centre of the garden, but the serpent, Satan, tries to convince the woman it would be quite logical to eat from this tree, because it did not seem to do any harm and would give knowledge. Whether it is an historical account of what happened or allegorical, the message seems very clear to me. The taunts of Satan, convincing us to disobey God, are the same today. 'Why should it be wrong? What harm can it do? Surely it is good for you!' The woman gave her husband the fruit and both took part in this disobedient act which we refer to as 'the Fall'. Sin had entered the world. The first results of this would seem to be an awareness of their own nakedness.

Their sexuality had become affected by sin, and was now deviant. The conclusion must be that none of us has a perfect or normal sexuality, if our standard is God's original ideal. We all fall short. Our fallen sexuality, whatever it may be, sometimes seeks expression in ways that are not honouring to God and are sinful. It may also be expressed in ways that are not sinful. Whatever the case, everyone's sexuality is affected by sin and therefore deviant to some degree.

The Church and Sodom

The debate in the Church has usually centred around whether relationships of love between two people of the same sex can involve genital sexual activity and still be honouring to God. The story of Sodom and Gomorrah in Genesis 19 is often used in this debate. This story, however, does not involve a loving act, but gang rape. In this respect it is not relevant to the current controversy, but in another way it is. Ezekiel 16:48–9 says that homosexual rape was not the only sin of Sodom. The cities also displayed a selfishness and lack of concern for the poor and needy. This also offended God.

Leviticus

In Leviticus 18, male homosexual activity is called an abomination to God. Some would argue that there are many prohibitions in Leviticus we take no notice of today – for example, the wearing of material woven from mixed fabrics. However, I believe there is a distinction between some of the culturally based prohibitions in Leviticus and the prohibitions on behaviour which is related to human nature. Human nature has not changed in terms of its basic desires and therefore the condemnation of behaviour like idolatry (putting anything or anyone before God), bestiality, incest, adultery, fornication and homosexuality must still be relevant today. Having said that, I might still have a lot of doubts about my theological position if it was based simply on these verses in Leviticus, but the Bible says a lot more.

Homosexuals and Heterosexuals Not in the Bible

Jesus does not mention homosexuality specifically, but I believe his dialogue with the disciples recorded in Matthew 19 is relevant to this debate. It is important to recognise that in biblical times, people were not identified by a sexual orientation in the way we are today. This has only been fashionable since the late nineteenth century. In other words, in Jesus' day, there was no such person as a homosexual or heterosexual, just people with many different sexual feelings and desires.

What Does Jesus Say?

When Jesus discusses the issue of divorce and remarriage with his disciples (Matt. 19:1–12), they respond by saying, 'If this is the case, it would be better not to be married.' This is a lovely reminder that the disciples were very real people. Then Jesus says clearly that not everyone will be married. He gives three overriding reasons why a person may not be married, each one encompassing a multitude of situations. The first one is genetic, possibly referring to factors that have limited the options for marriage, which have a genetic root. Second, he describes people who have possibly found it difficult to get married because of circumstances, emotional problems or sexual problems. He may have included in this people who were not attracted to the opposite sex sexually. Third, Jesus says that some will make a positive choice not to be married for the sake of the kingdom of heaven. However all these unmarried people, for whatever reason, are described by Jesus as eunuchs. This does not necessarily mean people who are physically castrated, but I think Jesus makes the assumption that unmarried people will not be involved in a sexual relationship. He would not need to qualify or explain this, because it would have been accepted teaching to his listeners.

When I became a committed Christian, it was looking at the life of Jesus Christ and the moral issues he addressed which convinced me that he would not be happy with my homosexual relationships. However, I never had any doubt that he loved me and accepted me as a person, understanding me completely, including my homosexual feelings and temptations.

The Apostle Paul

Paul is much more explicit about homosexual relationships. Romans 1 talks about men and women who exchange the truth of God for a lie and worship and serve the creature rather than the Creator. Paul lists homosexual relationships as one of the results of that exchange. He talks about it in terms of exchanging natural relations with the opposite sex for unnatural relations with the same sex.

Some Christians argue that when Paul uses the terms 'natural' and 'unnatural' he is talking about what is natural to the person in terms of his or her sexual orientation. It is therefore said that Paul is talking about people who are 'naturally' heterosexual getting involved in homosexual relationships which are 'unnatural' to them, as a part of the permissive promiscuous society in Rome. Similarly, it would be 'unnatural' for someone who only had homosexual feelings to be involved in a heterosexual relationship. This argument can be persuasive, especially if one is involved in a loving homosexual relationship, which can feel like the most natural thing in the world. However, when we look at Paul's words in the context of the first two chapters and indeed the whole book of Romans, it seems to me pretty clear that Paul is addressing the Fall and its implications for us.

The exchange he is referring to is the tendency within all of us to disobey God and exchange our 'vertical' relationship with him for 'horizontal' relationships with each other (no pun intended!). So when Paul is talking about 'natural' and 'unnatural', he is referring to what is natural to God and not necessarily what is natural to us. He goes on to list many other results or fruits of our disobedience to God – gossip, envy, disobedient children. Perhaps Paul used homosexual behaviour as the first example because his context was that of creation. He is in a way emphasising his point by using the example of homosexual relationships rather than adultery or fornication. However, it is important to realise that he is addressing all of us as people who have disobeyed God and therefore become involved in behaviour which is unnatural in terms of God's ideal. In Romans 2, he reminds us that we are all involved in this and guilty of the behaviour he has just highlighted. The book of Romans really addresses the truth of the gospel. It therefore makes sense that before Paul talks about his own battle with sin in Romans 7 and the wonderful truth of God's forgiveness and redemption, he should start from the beginning, by addressing the issue of the Fall.

It has been argued that Paul was not aware of homosexual relationships as we know them today. In biblical times, it was not uncommon for men to have a sexual relationship with younger teenage men. Is Paul really dealing just with this? No. He is clearly talking about men having sex with men, that is adults. It also seems to show a remarkable insight that he mentions lesbianism, which I understand was unusual for his time.

Paul also mentions homosexual behaviour in 1 Corinthians 6. This time it is listed alongside a lot of other behaviour which he says is incompatible with membership of the kingdom of heaven. The unusual word Paul uses is similar to the Greek translation of the Levitical prohibition. However, homosexual behaviour is listed alongside sins like greed, idolatry and pride. This is sinful behaviour which, if we are honest, none of us can deny expressing. Paul also reminds us that this behaviour has been dealt with at the cross of Christ. We can continually bring it to God and receive his forgiveness, as we seek to overcome it. He says we 'were washed, sanctified and justified'. The past tense is used to remind us that, if we struggle and even sin in these ways, God has ultimately redeemed us through the death of Jesus on the cross.

David and Jonathan

David and Jonathan's relationship is sometimes accused of being homosexual, because of the depth of their love for one another and the strong emotions expressed at their final meeting. Saul's anger and its threat to David's safety meant Jonathan and David had to part, while pledging their love and commitment to each other.

> *David got up from the south side of the stone and bowed down before Jonathan three times, with his face to the ground. Then they kissed each other and wept together – but David wept the most. Jonathan said to David, 'Go in peace, for we have sworn friendship with each other in the name of the Lord, saying, "The Lord is witness between you and me, and between your descendants and my descendants for ever"' (1 Sam. 20:41–2).*

The expression translated 'but David wept the most' in the New International Version is in the King James translation, 'until David exceeded'. It is argued that this could mean that David had an orgasm. This seems very unlikely bearing in mind the Old Testament prohibitions on homosexuality and adultery. If that were the case, it would surely have been given more significance. David's adultery with Bathsheba was certainly highlighted. If he had been involved in homosexual activity, it would surely have been mentioned.

However, this beautiful picture of same-sex love does show us that love, affection and commitment in relationships are not just for marriage. It is not beyond the realms of possibility that David and Jonathan may have been tempted sexually with each other, just as they may have been tempted to be jealous, self-centred, emotionally dependent or idolatrous in their relationship. Possibly, none of these were an issue, but we do not know for sure. I think in biblical times temptations, including sexual ones, would have been seen as present in many different forms for everyone, rather than just one particular group. In other words, people would not have been identified by a same-sex or homosexual orientation in the way we are today, as mentioned previously. It would not have been seen as totally out of the question for David and Jonathan to be attracted to each other or even tempted sexually, but they would not have been called 'homosexuals' or 'bisexuals' as they would today. Perhaps there would be less fear and prejudice if we were able to stop using the identity labels that society seems to demand.

Why Is It Wrong?

The Bible condemns any sexual relationship outside the 'one-flesh' relationship of marriage. Homosexual acts, adultery, fornication, incest, bestiality all fall outside this ideal. Sexual desires are as varied and different as the people with them. They have rarely been deliberately sought, but result from many influences, such as those mentioned in Chapter 3. Sexual feelings are 'natural' for the person with them and may involve a loving motive. Society rightly demands that some of these 'natural feelings', especially directed towards children, must not be expressed. The Bible gives much more restrictive boundaries. All of us will at times deny ourselves a sexual relationship, for social or biblical reasons. When social norms feel loving and seem to harm no one, it can be difficult to understand why the Bible says something different. This is often the case with homosexuality. Why should a homosexual relationship of love be wrong?

I believe we need to understand a little more about the mystery of a 'one-flesh' relationship. The creation narrative in Genesis 2 gives an account of the woman being created from the man. She is then united, or symbolically reunited with him. They are no longer two, but mysteriously 'one flesh'. We are also told this union must not be broken.

This prohibition is repeated throughout Scripture. This one-flesh marriage relationship is very important to God. Perhaps in one sense it symbolises the very act of his creation of man and woman? The orgasm experienced by the man and woman in sexual intercourse may have been intended to celebrate God's act of creation. God takes symbolism very seriously in his relationship with us. The Old and New Testaments make this clear. Perhaps sex outside marriage could be compared to taking the bread and wine at the Lord's Supper, simply because you like the taste of it? Surely it profanes the meaning of the symbolism and seriously offends God?

There is also the sense in which the 'one-flesh' relation-ship was intended as a lifelong commitment and potential family or procreative unit. Extramarital relationships seriously damage its stability. Any breakdown in this relationship hurts the Lord as well as the people involved.

The Bible prohibits sex outside marriage, of which homosexual relationships are one example. This seems to be for theological and sociological reasons. It offends God's sovereignty and love for his children. It is a form of idolatry, because it does not put God first.

However, many other sins, which appear more accept-able, are equally offensive for similar reasons. This is per-haps why sexual sins are always listed alongside pride, greed and envy. These are some of the greatest sins in the Church, and usually manifest themselves in their less obvious forms – for example, in a desire to appear 'spiritual' or religious.

Impossibly Demanding?

The biblical prohibition of sex outside marriage can seem impossibly demanding in a culture that says that sex is a natural expression of love, inside or outside marriage. The person with homosexual feelings sees people of the same sex all the time who sometimes stir tremendously strong emotions. It can seem cruel to deny this expression in any way. Many Christians feel condemned by God every time they are attracted to someone of the same sex. Is this necessary? I believe the answer to that is often, 'No'.

Satan uses Scripture, frequently, to accuse and condemn us. This includes the words of Jesus when he says if you have looked at a woman lustfully, you have already committed adultery with her in your mind and that is sin (Matt. 5:28). Jesus is first emphasising hypocrisy, but in any case is lust simply sexual attraction? Surely it is a much stronger emotion than sexual attraction or even desire? It is more of an obsessional craving for sex with a particular person and maybe even plotting ways in which that can be realised.

Attraction Need Not Mean Sex

I know in my own life I can find people of the same sex attractive at times, emotionally and physically, but that does not mean I want to pursue them to have sex. This is sexual attraction and I need to accept it, knowing only too well that if I make it a big issue, there could be problems of temptation or desire. If I do find myself in a situation of desiring sex with someone, I can choose not to follow it through.

I can even appreciate the beauty of another, without it becoming lustful. Obviously, anything like this can have its own control over me, which would be wrong, but that can apply to anything. Any object which attracts me, human or otherwise, can become an idol to me. That does not mean the attraction is wrong in itself, although my low self-image and perhaps the secrecy of my attractions will make me vulnerable ground to attack.

No to Sex – Yes to Love

A life without sex should not mean a life without love or awareness of the attractiveness of others. I have the incentive and the choice to make sure that attractions do not lead to sin, and that closeness and intimacy in relationships do not result in sex. My desire for this purity is an expression of my love for another person. That may sound crazy to some. It is certainly not what we are encouraged to believe these days, yet, I am saying that 'No to sex *is* yes to love!'.

Celibate and Sexually Faithful

Denying myself sex can seem like denying my humanity – but everyone denies themselves sex at times, whatever their moral framework. Before I became a Christian, I was able to be sexually faithful to a lover. That would mean denying myself sex at times and certainly meant that I stopped looking for it. As a Christian I am now seeking to be faithful to Jesus, morally and sexually, although I fail and need to experience his forgiveness.

Celibacy evokes negative feelings in me. It seems to describe a life of self-denial, with which I cannot identify. Perhaps that is my problem? Celibacy seems to deny sexuality, but this is not true. I may be seeking celibacy, but I am still a sexual person in the sense that anyone seeking to be faithful to a lover is. I am like many others in the Church. Statistically, there must be more Christians denying themselves heterosexual relationships and marriage, for Christ, than homosexual ones. It is often claimed that: 'Celibacy is a gift or calling for some', as if it is for special people. That is not true; we are all called to be faithful and obedient to Jesus Christ if we are seeking to follow his narrow road to everlasting life.

5

Free to Choose

I wrote in Chapter 2 about the gift of responsibility. It is a vital part of our value as human beings that we are free to choose and make our own mistakes, as well as make good choices. There are times when we may have responsibility for others, especially children or those who are mentally disabled in some way. However, when we love someone and want the best for that person, it can be so difficult to let go and let the loved one slide down what we may believe is a slippery slope. As a Christian I find seeking to trust the person to God's goodness can be a wonderful comfort. The problem is that I know this will not necessarily protect my loved one from more hurt and harm. Acknowledging the sovereignty of God and accepting that his ways do not fit my ideas of logic, or even sometimes justice, is very difficult. We will look at this again in the next chapter. I find I must cling to the truth that a freedom to choose means allowing a person self-worth and value. Therefore, letting go of another and giving that person responsibility, is a positive act of loving.

Moral Choices

I have already said what I believe the Bible says about homosexuality. You know the moral choices I make concerning my own sexuality. Many people find this very difficult to accept, both for others and themselves. When I speak to non-Christians and share my beliefs as sensitively as possible, there is often an angry response. I hate confrontation and for me this is a nightmare scenario. My opponents seem to believe I am demanding the same moral choices of them. Perhaps you were feeling like this when you read the last chapter about the Bible?

I have already mentioned some reasons why we may have strong feelings about this subject. Few of us like to be criticised, if we are honest. If I am saying something is wrong for me, the assumption will be that I am also saying it is wrong for you. I am, of course, but this does not necessarily mean I am criticising you in the sense of being judgmental. If I am loving you as a reflection of God's love, my feelings should be of understanding and empathy, but sadness as I see what I believe grieves God. Nevertheless, I should appreciate the ways in which I also grieve and offend God, longing for you to point them out to me. That can sound idealistic. In reality it may be very different. A low self-image is likely to make any of us react angrily towards just a hint of criticism. It can also make some feel even worse about themselves and simply confirm self-hatred. Some Christians have expressed a lot of fear and prejudice towards homosexuals and made many people understandably angry and resentful towards a Christian moral choice which therefore appears to encourage fear and prejudice or homophobia.

Loss of Identity

We have looked at the sense of loss and the pain of bereavement when a loved one discloses for the first time what is an important part of their identity. That person can feel like a stranger. The sense of loss is even greater when the lifestyle or moral choices of the loved one sharply contrast or conflict with our own moral choices. This may already be the case before we know about the sexuality issues, but when it involves the other person's changing direction it really can be devastating.

Many moral choices Christians make conflict sharply with public opinion. There is often a sense of solidarity and bonding with other Christians who share the same belief system. This is true for any strong ideology. Our beliefs and moral choices form an important part of our sense of identity. Bonding with a loved one with a similar belief system brings a sense of security and in a way becomes a part of our own identity. I am not trying to say that we should not affirm our own uniqueness, but the sense of 'not being alone' is met to some extent by others sharing a similar lifestyle. This is strengthened when we have both invested a lot of emotional capital in the relationship. This was certainly Delroy's experience when Rachel left her faith as well as her marriage. Similarly, when Carol's friend Mary changed her theological viewpoint, she seemed a different person as far as Carol was concerned.

True to Myself

Several times in my own life as a Christian, people close to me have abandoned their Christianity and become involved in gay sexual relationships. Statements like, 'I need to be true to myself!' are often made. In such circumstances I usually experience many mixed feelings. They vary in intensity depending on my depth of love and commitment for the other person. There is always a tremendous sense of sadness. This once developed into clinical depression. Frustration and helplessness are also high on my agenda, and some jealousy at times. The frustration often centres around not fully identifying with the feelings of the loved one.

For example, throughout my experience as a Christian, I have always felt I was being true to myself – no matter how close or distant, obedient or disobedient I was being as a Christian. Until very recently I have simply not been able to even understand, let alone identify with, Christians who feel they are not being true to themselves. We will look at this issue again in the next chapter.

If I am really honest with myself, I also at times feel angry with a loved one who abandons Christianity. I feel betrayed, to some extent. I realise this is irrational and not justified, but it is a feeling I have to own, even though it seems unfair to the loved one, who is also hurting. They may wish it could be different.

There may be a desire to please and even a temptation to agree with my belief system in order to be accepted. That would be totally wrong and a deformation of my loved one's self-worth and freedom. Some of us have based our sense of self-value on living to please others. Christianity may be perceived as encouraging this process. Dying to self and living for others is at the heart of following Christ. However, believing our worth is dependent on that is not honouring God. It is denying our intrinsic value as creations of our Creator. How easy it is to pervert basic Christian truths when we have a low opinion of our value to God and other people. Our loved one may be affirming their own sense of worth by rejecting a Christianity which they feel destroys this. This is not true Christianity, but perceptions are born from a lifetime of messages, often misunderstood. Maybe our loved one will discover, through Christ, the 'truth which sets free'. Maybe we will discover that for ourselves as we seek to love them.

Freedom to Choose

Both of us have been given by God a freedom to make our own choices. It is a part of our value as human beings. What if we feel the choice our loved one has made is the wrong one?

Perhaps the mistake we believe this person has made is one we have made ourselves and have learnt through it? There can be a feeling of desperation as we long to convince the loved one of this. Our attempts may be met with strong resistance. On the other hand, advice may be accepted. This could be to please us or it may come from a real conviction that we are right. Is there a right and wrong way to respond? Do we simply leave well alone and perhaps just pray? What happens when our loved one's moral choice affects us in a practical way? For example, if we are unhappy about a sexual relationship, do we allow the partners to sleep together in our house? There are no easy answers. The uniqueness of each situation and the people involved make it impossible to offer any blueprint for a way forward. However, there are some basic principles within which we can try to move ahead.

Communication

Having sought to become aware of our feelings, having honestly tried to understand them and identified what is rational and irrational, we may be able to communicate them. This should be a mutual exchange in which we convey as much as possible about what is going on inside us. The temptation to interrupt each other must be resisted and every effort made to listen effectively, without constantly worrying about how we are going to respond to what is being said.

I remember being on a silent retreat, where I spent several hours on my own with God and myself. I was seeking to listen both to my own feelings and God's response to them. We met in groups to state, if we wished, what had been happening to each of us in this internal dialogue. However, no one was allowed to respond verbally to what had been shared. There was no discussion allowed. I found the effect of this astonishing. I could clearly remember what had been said with a clarity that I had rarely experienced in other groups where discussion is encouraged. As I saw other members of the retreat at various times during the week, they seemed much more 'real', much more 'known' to me than I would have thought possible. I wondered why this should be, when we had not been baring our souls intensively in group therapy? I came to the conclusion that it was probably because we were all seeking to be real with ourselves internally, and before God. I was not concerned about how I was going to respond to the feelings of others, whether I would say the right or wrong thing. This gave a wonderful sense of freedom and acceptance to the group.

Some of us are better at communicating and listening than others, but we can all work at it. *I believe it is very important to share not only the feeling, but how I feel about sharing it.* Once we feel we have both shared our feelings, it is often unhelpful to keep recommunicating them. I may be tempted to keep raising an issue, like a dog returning to an old bone.

We All Have Moral Choices

The focus can often be on acceptance of the loved one's moral choices, but we also have a right to be accepted for our own moral choices. Mark and Tony were very much aware of this as they related to Mark's parents, Pat and Richard. Mark clearly respected his parents' Christian beliefs and knew they would have a problem affirming his homosexual relationship because of this. He made this clear when he told Pat and Richard that he and Tony had not had sex in their house when they stayed there. This was before his parents knew about his sexual relationship and it proved his tremendous integrity. This was an act of love towards his parents, which meant a lot to them. Richard and Pat wondered if they should not put this restriction on their son. After all, it seemed something of a technicality. Mark and Tony's sexual activity was for them an important part of their relationship and expression of love for one another. Richard and Pat shared their feelings with Mark. He was touched that this should even be questioned by his parents. His response was that, whilst he wished they were as happy as he was with his relationship, he respected their beliefs and would still seek to refrain from sex with Tony when in their house. It might be tempting to believe this showed an underlying questioning in Mark's mind about his relationship, but not necessarily. Maturity, understanding and integrity on Mark's part were in my opinion expressed here.

What if the loved one is a Christian and yet accepting as right a relationship that we believe to be wrong? This was the situation with Carol and her friend Mary, who felt her lesbian relationship was honouring to God. Do we continue the relationship as if nothing was happening? Again we must seek to be honest with ourselves about what we are feeling. It can be very tempting to maintain the status quo in the hope that our love and acceptance will win the day and convince the loved one that they are wrong.

Do Not Orchestrate

I have tried at times carefully to orchestrate situations and the people in them to see if they can change their mind. Is this really God's way? I find it difficult to believe it is. I remember a mum who used carefully to plan social events so that her sons would be exposed to a positive Christian witness. Thankfully, they knew exactly what she was doing and had a good sense of humour. She was delightfully eccentric and we all used to find ourselves giggling help-lessly at the situation.

I know I have been just as unsubtle in trying to bring a loved one back to God's way, as I perceived it. I have organised trips to Christian concerts, only to feel even more frustrated when the barriers to accepting God's love seem to be even reinforced, rather than, as I had hoped, come tumbling down. As someone from a homosexual background I do not have a problem accepting a non-Christian involved in gay relationships.

At times I do find it difficult to relax with gay people who I feel will think I am strange. This is probably because of the hostility I often receive because of my Christian beliefs and moral choices. I know many of my Christian friends do not have this kind of problem. I can work through it as I get to know the other person and they know me. In some situations I can eventually feel comfortable with non-Christian friends. However, with other close friends in a similar position I feel quite differently.

A Personal Problem of Law and Love

I hope it is not self-indulgent if I write something of a conflict I have experienced and with which you may identify. It illustrates the need to work with principles of God's love, rather than rigid legalism. I cannot claim to be right. Many would disagree with my approach, but I can only share my feelings and responses to this situation, as they actually were at the time.

A close friend invited me to his parties. Sometimes the atmosphere in terms of conversations and behaviour highlighted for me the choice my friend had made to stop following Christ. I found this hurt me in many ways. The sense of identity and unity of spirit we had once experienced seemed abused, although not totally lost. I believe Jesus was also hurt. I had very mixed feelings, some of which I hope reflected Jesus's feelings. Others may have involved some jealousy. I struggled to identify the legitimate ones. I had to make a choice when invited to these parties. Did I accept in order to avoid offending anyone, especially my friend, or did I not? It was a decision always preceded by much heart-searching and confusion.

I knew my feelings were not a reflection of my acceptance or disapproval of my friend's friends. Most of them I would describe as nice people. If it was a question of simply meeting them there would not be a problem, apart from fears of their feelings about me. Similarly, there would not be a problem if my Christian friend was still following Christ. I realised the real issue for me was my friend's relationship with Jesus. This may sound strangely 'super-spiritual' and you may be tempted to ask, 'Is this real, or just an excuse for fear, prejudice and jealousy?' As I said before, I could not deny an element of these, but I know I can deal with them.

To take jealousy, for example; before I was a Christian I frequently experienced unrequited love and was able to relate to both the loved one and his lover. I know I have the capacity to do this. However, the spiritual issue with people I love seems to provoke feelings I had not known before I became a Christian. The barrier my friend seemed to have put up between himself and God frightened me. I believed God would never reject him, but my concern was about a hardness in my friend's heart. One evening he sensed my depression and asked what it was about. Reluctantly I tried to explain I was scared he might never return to God, for the reasons I have just mentioned. As I spoke my voice started to falter and then I wept uncontrollably. My friend had never seen me weep like this. It was unusual indeed. I will never forget the experience because I knew I was not weeping for myself. It seemed out of my own control.

A year later my friend invited me to a party with his gay friends and I was going through the usual emotional turmoil. I told him about my mixed feelings. A part of me wanted to be there for his sake and to please him, but I knew it would not be a pleasant experience. I would find it depressing, because it would make me aware of how far he was distancing himself from God. I knew I could pretend to be enjoying myself, making the evening a painful experience for me. Would this not make me a hypocrite? At one point he did say I was one of the people he most wanted to be there. Should I therefore say, 'Yes' – simply for his sake?

What would it achieve? He would know how I was truly feeling and therefore feel self-conscious. Eventually he agreed he only wanted me to be there, if I also wanted to be there. I could not honestly say I did. He respected my feelings.

It was probably right for me not to go, simply because I would have felt the need to be dishonest about my feelings. This may sound strange, and I am not saying it would have been right for all his Christian friends to react in the same way. It is not a reflection on their own spirituality. I believed it to be an expression of my love for him. I would not have refused to go on the basis of his friends' lifestyles. I would probably not have refused to go simply on the basis of how it reminded me about his relationship with God. It was because of my love for him and I think he accepted that. I hope this was because we communicated our feelings to each other. I realised this would make it unlikely for him to share any problems he was experiencing in his relationships, because he might have seen me as unsympathetic. I would have been sympathetic in the sense of hurting with him, but could not expect him to realise this.

His own emotional make-up made it difficult to receive criticism. It hurt too much. My unhappiness about his lifestyle, based on his relationship with God and my love for him, was difficult for him to handle. It was probably perceived at times as criticism and disapproval. In a sense it was, but the anger associated so often with criticism was for me replaced by sadness. It was not legalistic, but an expression of my love, which I recognise is often imperfect. I believe I understand him and his feelings, even if I have not experienced them all, but I cannot expect him to appreciate this. At times this has made me feel I failed him, because there is much he has felt unable to share with me.

Can a Moral Choice without Christ Work?

The answer must be, 'Yes'. Many people find a lot of happiness and fulfilment within homosexual relationships. They are not necessarily being socially immoral in terms of their love and concern for fellow human beings. In fact, sadly, they may be experiencing a lot more love within their relationships than they would within the Church. We can fall into the trap of trying to convince people that homosexual and lesbian relationships are wrong because they will never work out in the long term. This is not necessarily true. There are obviously emotional risks but not inevitable failure. Many Christians involved in HIV or AIDS work have been impressed by the quality of some gay relationships, often seeming to put heterosexual relationships to shame.

The most important moral choice we all have to make is whether to follow Christ or not. If I were not a Christian, I would be happily involved in gay relationships and believe them to be in most cases good for me.

What if My Loved One Believes a Gay Relationship Is Christian?

My first response is to say I wish I could agree, but I cannot. I believe it offends God, no matter how loving and good it may appear to be. A Christian who believes homosexual relationships with sexual expression are not compatible with Christianity has, I think, a difficult moral choice in terms of responding to this situation. Many would argue that the Bible's teaching is quite clear: *'You must not associate with anyone who calls himself a brother but is sexually immoral or greedy, an idolater or a slanderer, a drunkard or a swindler'* (*1 Cor 5:11*). They would say one should not have fellowship with Christians who proclaim such behaviour is not condemned by God. However, how many of us can claim to be totally obedient to God? Surely we all compromise in many ways and convince ourselves we are not disobeying God. How many of us are overweight and yet continue to indulge in overeating, without confessing it?

Perhaps the key lies in the underlying reasoning behind the Apostle Paul's words. His motivation is to prevent others in the body of Christ following in the same footsteps. In other words, a church will signal both to believers and unbelievers what it perceives as right or wrong. If wrong behaviour is ignored, people will believe it to be acceptable.

The Grace of Excommunication

Paul sees it as an act of love for Christians to distance themselves from fellow believers who are disobedient. Through denying them fellowship, he is hoping they will be encouraged honestly to come to realise their behaviour is wrong. This has been called, 'The grace of excommunication'. Rather than drifting along in compromise, a person is encouraged to be alone with moral choices and therefore hopefully forced to face the issues. You may remember this was the situation with Jennifer and her mother who sexually abused her and yet would not accept responsibility.

Communication and Discipline – Not Punishment

Communication is again the key. If we are struggling about how to respond in such a situation, we should talk about it. There may be some cases where it is right to withdraw from the relationship, but if this is so, we must be honest with ourselves and the loved one. I remember someone using the expression, 'I do this so reluctantly and with tears in my eyes. There seems no alternative!' I believe it illustrates the godly motivation of love, which must rule in these painful choices. The opportunity for reconciliation must always be there. I can honestly say in over fifteen years of meeting Christians who have been disciplined by their church, I cannot clearly remember any situation in which I have believed the discipline to be justified, according to scriptural principles. They have been expressions of punishment and prejudice, generally speaking, rather than loving godly discipline. The Christians on the receiving end had been thoroughly convinced their behaviour was dishonouring to God and were longing to experience freedom from temptation and sin.

Reconciliation

God's love is continually seeking reconciliation with his children. No matter how hardened our hearts become, the love of our Lord Jesus is seeking to break through and communicate. If our love is to mirror God's, we should do all in our power to enable the loved one to receive his love and forgiveness. There is no blueprint for this. The way of reconciliation for one may not be the same for another. It will be different for Christians, than for non-Christians. It may involve fellowship, or withdrawal of it. It may involve meeting our loved one's non-Christian friends, or not. *It will always need honesty and prayerful consideration.*

6

Healing and Comfort

The word 'healing' means so many things to different people. Some gay people find it offensive because they believe it implies homosexuality is an illness to be cured. It is similar to their reaction to homosexuality being called a sin. Most gays and lesbians who are happy and fulfilled in their lifestyle see homosexual behaviour as an important part of their self-worth and identity. Words like 'sin' and 'healing' are understood to imply unacceptability as people. But what do we really mean by 'healing'? An initial starting point is that it means 'wholeness' – 'completeness' as a person. I understand that is an accurate biblical interpretation of the word. It certainly sounds right, but is still not clearly defined. I guess the truth is that healing will have different meanings in different situations, but always implies a sense of wellbeing and fulfilment with oneself and others. I would also say that Christian healing has a major distinction, because the person concerned is aware of God in the process and has a truthful, fulfilling, secure relationship with the Creator.

Healing for Us All

I hope as you read this you are not simply thinking of a desire for healing in your loved one. That would have been my only response at one time. It was also an expression of my own lack of healing. Obviously, we want the best for those we love, but if we can only see their need for healing, rather than our own, we have a problem. *I believe healing should be seen as a process for all of us in all relationships and experiences.*

The last ten years of my own life have taught me more about God, others and myself than ever before, through hurts and frustrations as well as joys. I have often been forced by circumstances and sometimes other people to accept situations and work through them with God's help. That does not mean bad situations are necessarily transformed into good ones, but it does mean I can become richer through them. I am not saying that tragedy and pain in the lives of others is a blessing for me. Tragic circumstances and hurting people can never be described in anything less than negative terms. If I am privileged to share in someone else's pain, it must also hurt me. It will help me understand and identify with the pain of others. I may experience a new understanding of myself, as sharing in the pain of others brings to the surface issues of hurt and pain in my own life. I could discover sinful responses in myself which make me aware of my own weakness and lead me to become less judgmental. I may be challenged to love. I will need to work at my relationship with God, other people and even myself in new ways. These have been aspects of healing in my own life and can be in the lives of my loved ones also, if allowed to be so. I must emphasise that this does not mean we should try to convince ourselves that 'It didn't hurt' or 'It wasn't bad.' I believe tragedy and joy should be seen in the context of the larger picture of our life's journey. The areas of healing and comfort I want to outline are for us all, whatever our sexuality.

Receiving Love and Forgiveness

Undoubtedly the most important part of the healing process involves receiving love and forgiveness. A secular philosopher once remarked: 'The only remedy for the inevitability of our history is forgiveness.' The head of a large mental hospital said: 'I could dismiss half of my patients tomorrow if they could be assured of forgiveness.' So many ways in which we express ourselves, emotionally and sexually, are driven by low self-esteem. Even what appears to be a 'big ego' may in reality be the opposite. We have defence mechanisms which attempt to convince others and even ourselves that we are not what we believe ourselves to be. These defences are saying something about the way we see ourselves and other people. 'I want you to tell me I'm acceptable.' 'I wish I was like you.' 'I hate you because you are like me.' 'How dare you tell me what to do?' 'I am the best.'

Perfectionism

One of the fruits of a low self-image is perfectionism. I demand perfection of myself and usually of others. It must all work out for me in a logical way. Failure is painful. Even the process of growth and healing becomes yet another perfectionist exercise. Terminology like 'programs' and even the word 'healing' can imply success and failure. A vicious circle often develops. I feel a failure, and seek a comfort to make me feel better. This may be through behaviour which I believe is wrong. I therefore return to the sense of failure and seek a comfort once more. A reaction to this continual sense of failure is sometimes to abandon many of the moral boundaries I set myself. I believe this will break the vicious circle of failure – guilt – comfort, then back to failure, which keeps repeating itself. However, I will probably still not be satisfied. I will still search for perfection and the hunger will never feel completely satiated. *This cycle may be part of an obsessional compulsive personality. There is also likely to be a tendency to addiction. This can be to sex, relationships, drugs or ideologies.* Abandoning Christianity will not mean an end to this. It may simply be expressed in different ways.

Addiction

Addiction must be owned and worked at, in whatever form it appears. Sex and relationship addictions are not always seen in the same way as other addictions, but they should be. Many Christians and non-Christians have been helped by sexuality – and relationship – addiction groups, based on the Twelve Steps of Alcoholics Anonymous. It can be very helpful for people with homosexual struggles to work alongside others struggling in very similar ways with heterosexuality.

An addictive problem can be a response to the deeper problems we work at in the healing process, but it should be treated as an issue in itself. It is a bit like dealing with an irritating rash or acne and at the same time working to change my diet or inner tensions, which may have caused it. *The apparent paradox is to own and accept the addiction, yet work through it at the same time as the underlying causes.*

Otherwise the circle of guilt – comfort – guilt cannot be broken.

Perfection

A perfectionist may be attracted to Christianity because it appears to offer perfection, or at least the possibility of attaining it. The ethos of never failing seems to be linked with acceptability and being lovable. The flaws in this ideology may be acknowledged, in theory, but ignored in experience.

God is the only source of perfect love, which is not perfectionistic in the sense we may experience perfection. The standards of love expressed in 1 Corinthians 13 are not perfectionist. They keep 'no record of wrongs' and 'do not envy'. We need to repent of perfectionism, because in a sense it is a form of idolatry. We are demanding to be just like God and therefore in no need of his forgiveness, through Christ's death on the cross. Our hurts, fears and insecurities have made us into perfectionists, but they are not an excuse to permit it. Christianity may have become yet another perfectionist exercise. Healing is perceived as success and failure is devastating. A conviction of sin is often disappointed perfectionism and therefore leads to godless repentance.

Receiving Forgiveness

This is the only way to deal with perfectionism, because I am recognising and accepting my imperfection and failures. I also seek to resolve them in order that they cease to control my sense of self-worth. It is only from God and through him that I can experience complete forgiveness. This is an ongoing process throughout my life. That sounds idealistic, and experiencing the reality of this perfect love and forgiveness is something we all find difficult. The gospel, or good news, of God's love and forgiveness has become perverted, to some extent. It actually makes us feel worse when we fail, rather than redeemed, because we have not felt forgiven. The baggage of life experiences we carry with us affects all relationships and our responses to them, especially a relationship with God.

Distorted Image of God

We have a distorted or imperfect image of God which inhibits our ability to receive his love.

- God may seem to be a demanding parent who will only accept me and therefore love me if I am perfect.
- God may seem distant and remote because that is what I have been conditioned to expect of him.
- God may seem to be 'Santa Claus' who gives me anything I want if I shout loud enough or do enough good deeds.
- God may even seem to be the ultimate perfectionist who always makes everything work out perfectly, because he is thoroughly logical and explicable.

These are all distorted images of God that we have received as a result of our own relationships in life, and the Church has often encouraged such distortion.

Accepting Mystery and Paradox

Society today denies any mystery about life. We must have answers for everything. The 'instant fix' social norm has influenced the Church and our own individual spirituality. We believe God's ways should be logical, explicable, without any paradox. Problems should ultimately be fixed, and black turned into white. We will use Scriptures like Romans 8:28: '*And we know that in all things God works for the good of those who love him*' to mean everything should come right. It does mean this, but not necessarily according to *our* definition of what 'right' means. For example, when the apostle Paul tells us about his 'thorn in the flesh' he describes it as a messenger of Satan sent by God to stop him from being too elated. Paul adds that God's power was made perfect through his weakness.

My logical mind finds it difficult to understand how a loving God who wants the best for us could possibly send something apparently satanic. God is sovereign and therefore in ultimate control of evil. God is also the only one who is completely good. How can my limited human mind understand what seems illogical?

Perhaps this all happened so that God could prove himself by rescuing Paul from this satanic messenger? His power was being made perfect by bringing Paul through this. That sounds much more logical. However, if we look at this in the context of Paul's life and place in God's kingdom, not anticipating a logical conclusion, it may seem different. Perhaps Paul had a tendency to be a bit judgmental as a Pharisee? He needed a 'thorn' (a problem, certainly, maybe even a sin?) to stop him from being too elated and judgmental. Maybe Paul's thorn was one reason he could talk about himself as the 'worst of sinners' (1 Tim. 1:16). Paul's thorn made him more 'whole' and enabled him to minister to others. That is how God's power was made perfect in Paul's weakness – in sending the problem and being within it, rather than in Paul's victory over it, which may never have happened. Paul's 'thorn' and his spiritual battles, fighting against his sinful nature – sometimes winning, sometimes losing – were all a part of his growth and healing. Perfect freedom was only experienced after his life on Earth.

What Has This to Do with Homosexuality in Family and Friends?

Low self-worth is one of the main contributors to homosexual feelings and probably a major driving force in anyone's life and relationships. If I want to work at my self-worth and my relationships with others, I cannot do better than learn to relate to God – the perfect lover. He will also teach me how to love and forgive others and how to receive forgiveness from them.

Learning to Receive God's Love

We learn to receive God's love as we learn to listen to him and to ourselves. I find one of the most effective ways of doing this is consciously to share my thoughts and feelings with the Lord and then allow myself to hear his response. This must be based on a knowledge of his nature, as revealed in Scripture, rather than my almost inevitably distorted image of it. I use my mind, rather than my feelings, to receive God's word for me. I know the Lord is aware of all my thoughts and feelings. One of the great mysteries of God's nature is the fact that he knows everything about everyone. I cannot hope to understand that, so I just have to accept it.

My act of sharing everything with the Lord, including my anger, frustration, doubts and fears about him and others, is saying that I trust him, albeit hesitantly. God is the only one with whom we can be totally safe to disclose everything. I also need to allow myself to receive the Lord's response. This is often the most difficult step, even though it may sound ridiculously simple. My own misconceptions about God and myself are almost certainly the major cause of this problem. I may find it difficult to feel that God wants to communicate with me so personally. I may allow myself to receive something of what God is saying to me, but it becomes tainted and distorted by my own feelings.

Examples of Listening – Tainted and Truthful

For example, I might pray: 'Lord, I wish I was a better person so that your power could be seen in my life!' The response I allow myself to receive could be: 'You know if you confess your sins I can forgive you and my power will be seen in your life when I have dealt with your sin.' Is God's grace and power quite so conditional? There is some truth expressed there, but it is slightly tainted by my low self-worth and rationality. Perhaps God's response, received more accurately, would be: 'I love you more than you can ever fully know, Martin, here on Earth. My power is made perfect in your weakness.'

I use my mind and knowledge of God's nature to receive that response of truth from God, rather than my feelings, many of which are based on misunderstandings and lies. Often, I will just allow myself to receive words like, 'I love you, Martin.' 'I am here with you.' These are basic truths which I cannot deny as being from God. How could I possibly question that God would want me to hear those words of truth? He knows me better than anyone else and therefore calls me by my name.

Going through this procedure can be quite a discipline for some of us. We may be tempted to doubt that what we receive is from God, because our minds have been used in the exercise. Surely, God is in our minds too. There will be times when God speaks to us without conscious effort on our part. There will also be times when we rightly question what we are receiving, in case it is not from God.

Power in Weakness

I am glad that in my own life and ministry I have seen God use me, when I felt this would be the last thing he would do because of my disobedience. If I had the option to avoid giving him the opportunity to do this, I would have done so. I would have backed out of situations and then not had the chance to be amazed at God's love and graciousness. As I get used to this communication process, I find my receiving a response from God becomes like a reflex action. I feel much safer with him. I long to have the space to unload my feelings, these days. Whenever I went on a long journey in the past, I always felt I needed entertaining to avoid boredom. I would use cassettes or the car radio to help the time pass. Now I often long for the silence, so I can bring thoughts and feelings to the surface, knowing that God is listening. *The Lord Jesus becomes my best friend as I learn to feel secure with him.* In fact he is the only one I can totally trust, who will never misunderstand or forsake me.

Listening and Healing

As I work at learning to listen to my loved one, to myself and to God, I am experiencing healing. There will be many issues that come to the surface in this listening process for me, personally, quite apart from my loved one. I may find feelings surface of which I was totally unaware. It may be that in simply being involved in this situation, I become a part of a whole spectrum of human experience. Though I have never experienced the situation myself, nevertheless it becomes a part of me, a part of my own identity.

This has certainly been true in my case. Without being married I can now understand at least something of how a wife feels when her husband leaves her. Without being a husband, I can identify with husbands who have felt a sense of failure and inadequacy that seemed intolerable – who have felt the pain and guilt of leaving those they love, because there seemed no alternative. Without being the child of a homosexual parent, I can identify with something of the loss when a father leaves home and the pain of seeing your loved ones apparently hurting each other and feeling helpless to respond. Having experienced so many of my own loved ones apparently rejecting Christianity for a homosexual lifestyle, I can identify with something of the pain of parents who have felt the apparent loss of a son or daughter in this way. I also know something of the joy when a loved one returns to Christ as a richer person.

All this and many other experiences are a part of my value now as a person in God's kingdom. This value can be measured in many different ways, not simply in understanding others – although that is a major part – but also in terms of understanding myself and God. It will make me look again at my own moral choices as a Christian, both for my own life and in the way I respond to the moral choices of others. This is all healing, even though it must often be difficult to recognise it as such at the time.

Healing for My Loved One

The process of healing for my loved one has to be that person's own choice. However, it may be helpful to know of possible ways forward in case advice is sought. Once again the principles are true for all of us. I have already discussed many of them. The healing processes for the homosexual and heterosexual are the same, yet experienced differently in each person.

First is an understanding of the nature of God and who he is. Our image of God as mentioned earlier and the choice or decision to go his way must come first. Then I need to work out with myself and God what I believe he says about my moral choices.

I must work at experiencing his love and forgiveness both for myself and others. This too has been mentioned, but it needs to be emphasised as the most important part of my healing process. Many components of my hurts, fears and insecurities will be worked at and this will affect the way I relate to myself and to others. It may in some cases even bring a change in my sexual feelings. Some find heterosexual feelings are experienced for the first time as they relate in a different way to people of the same and opposite sex. Others find homosexual feelings remain, but, as I keep emphasising, wholeness involves accepting all of these possibilities. In other words, perhaps healing is being experienced when it does not matter what the precise outcome is. The driving force behind sexual feelings of any sort is the need for love, both giving and receiving it.

7

Sexuality and Spirituality

Special Friendships

Whatever situation you are in, whatever relationship has
motivated you to read all this, you need to talk about your
own feelings with someone you can trust to keep confi-
dences. You need a close friend who understands you and
the way you feel and react. This is not always so easy to
experience. We all need those special friends who listen
and help us listen to ourselves. Advice givers and 'Job's
Comforters' are not so helpful. I know many people who
are discovering the wonderful ministry of listening. The
Acorn Christian Healing Trust have courses designed to
help us listen to others, ourselves and God. Listening is a
vital part of the healing process.

So many people who contact me say they have never
shared these issues with anyone else. That puts me in a
privileged position, but it should not have to be like that.
The Church, as the body of Christ, should consist of loving,
supporting, trusting relationships. The need for ministries
like TfT is in many ways a reflection on the lack of love
within many churches. The healing potential of love within
the body of Christ must be there for all of us, if we seek to

find it. I have mentioned the importance of listening to our loved ones and encouraging them to listen to us, but we also need to be listened to outside these relationships.

The Special Friend

The way we befriend or love one another should be a reflection of God's love, but it will also be influenced by our own feelings. Some of these will be mature, well-balanced and healthy, but others will be expressions of hurts, fear and insecurities within us. Sometimes we are aware of this and compensate accordingly, but often unhelpful emotions are expressed unconsciously. Jesus Christ is the only friend I can relate to, who does not have this problem. *Jesus calls me his friend and asks me to become his friend, also.*

> *Greater love has no-one than this, that one lay down his life for his friends. You are my friends if you do what I command. I no longer call you servants, because a servant does not know his master's business. Instead, I have called you friends, for everything that I learned from my Father I have made known to you (John 15:13–15).*

God, through Jesus, is the perfect lover and the perfect listener. This is one of the paradoxes or so-called myster- ies of God. The Lord is the only one who knows more about the situation and the feelings of all involved than anyone else. Why then, one may ask, do I need to tell him what he already knows? Sharing with Jesus, as a friend, is an act of worship. I am expressing to my Creator love and trust. I should feel safer to share with him than anyone else. I am showing him my awareness of his omnipresence. The Psalms give some wonderful examples of feelings expressed to God, even anger and disillusionment. It is interesting to see how many questions are answered by the psalmist about God as he listens to himself, the Holy Spirit and the human mind working in harmony. *This is incarnational reality – humanity and God working together.*

Incarnational Reality

This experience is the key to our growth. Healing involves being aware of God in every situation and allowing ourselves to hear him speak to us through it. This process conflicts with a logical human image of God. God hates suffering, but allows it. He hates sin, but allows it. How can my limited mind possibly cope with the idea that God allows me to sin, even when it is an abomination to him? In the same way, the question of suffering keeps cropping up. 'How can a God who loves me allow such tragedy to happen to me?' There are no simple answers, even though we may be tempted to manufacture them. Surely the only way forward must be to accept the paradox and my inevitably limited understanding of it. I accept the truth of the situation and my feelings, but recognise that whatever is happening to me and around me is a part of my life's story. In fact it is God's story with me. Just as in biblical times, whatever happens in my life has value for me and others. This includes the good and the bad, joy and tragedy, righteousness and sin.

The Split between Spirituality and Sexuality

I find one of the major problems for many Christians is the split between their humanity, sexuality and spirituality. This is one of the main reasons for the desperate frustration, which says, 'I must express my sexuality. I have to be true to myself.' We are conditioned to believe that sex is a natural bodily function that must be expressed. If I feel my Christianity is denying me this right, it seems like an impossible cross to bear. The very strong emotional feelings that we call sexuality also seem naturally linked to our sense of identity. We may be tempted to look for an equally powerful feeling or experience in the attempt to smother our sexual feelings and desires. If our spirituality is mainly experiential, in the sense of expecting manifestations and demonstrations of God's power, it may help us to deny sexual feelings. It may also help our Christian identity to feel more real, but our spirituality is then *only* associated with godly feelings and passions; while human feelings, including sexuality, are likely to be completely split off from spirituality.

This is not incarnational reality and limits my experience of healing and is likely to cause the abandonment of my spirituality in an effort to be true to my humanity. It is as if I am saying: 'This (my humanity) is who I am, but my spirituality does not allow me to be it.' This was certainly the way Rachel felt when she left her husband and Christianity for her relationship with Ella. The battle between her sexuality and spirituality had raged for years. She felt the only way to resolve this conflict was to abandon one of them. She had tried smothering the homosexual part of her sexuality, but the pain this caused when she seemed to fail became unbearable. Carol's friend, Mary, tried to repair the split by changing her theology to accommodate the desires of her heart. How many of us compromise in other areas of our lifestyles?

Healing the Split

If only I can allow myself to know God in all of my life, then my humanity, including sexuality, has value. Perhaps this becomes easier if we try to drop the sexual compart-mentalisation and just accept ourselves as sexual/emotional human beings. That means being aware of feelings, good and bad, but accepting they have value in what they tell us about ourselves and others. It is not attempting to make a bad or sinful experience seem not quite so bad, or even good. It is accepting that whatever happens in our lives is a part of our unique story and has some purpose and meaning in the bigger perspective of God's story. He is sovereign and has therefore allowed the experience. This is *the* incredible mystery, that God allows even what he hates and longs for us to overcome. Any life experiences can therefore be a catalyst to loving and understanding God, others and ourselves. They are an expression of our humanity and spirituality.

This must include our sexuality and means we are expressing sexuality, even when we are not having sex with anyone. It is a part of our unique emotional make-up and humanity. It has been suggested that allowing ourselves to know God speaking to us, even through sin, is like taking grace for granted and 'being soft on sin'. This should not be the case if we are working at this truthfully. We should actually experience more of God's love and more awareness of sin. It should be more difficult for me to sin when I cannot ignore that God is there. *The more I know my sin, the more I should experience God's love and forgiveness.*

The Past in the Present

Sometimes feelings and reactions in the present are a reaction to much more than the present situation. A relationship or experience of today may provoke an unusually strong response. It may seem out of proportion and unreasonable. It may appear unconnected with the past. However, it has triggered a response like anger, fear or insecurity which is really coming from an experience or relationship in the past. Recognising this in oneself can be an important way of working at it and therefore a catalyst to growth and healing. Seeing it in loved ones may help them, if they also understand what is really being expressed.

Not Good to Be Alone

It can be tempting to feel that I will only feel less 'alone' when I have other people and especially a one-to-one relationship. There is much truth in that, but 'aloneness' is not just a need for a life partner. It is a spiritual need, also. I must learn to be alone with myself and with God in the way I have tried to describe – knowing God in everything and listening to myself and him. This is often called 'listening prayer'. As I experience security in this way, so I can relate to others.

- As I learn to receive God's love, I learn to believe I am worth loving.
- As I learn to experience God in every area of my life, I see something of my part in God's story. I feel secure with myself and him.
- I can then more securely experience relationships that reflect my relationship with God. They must involve commitment, security and honesty. I need these special relationships of deep love. They will certainly have problems, including temptations and sins of many sorts. These can, at times, be catalysts for growth.

No to Sex Is Not No to Love

A life without sex should not mean a life without love for anyone. It can be tempting to believe that Christians with a homosexual orientation have a heavier cross to bear than their heterosexual counterparts. This should not be the case. Statistically, there are more Christians who deny themselves a heterosexual relationship because of their Christianity. I am grateful that during my first few years as a Christian I met many people in this situation. If I had suggested that at least they had a choice, it would have seemed incredibly cruel. They longed to settle down and raise a family, but no Christian partners were available, despite many attempts through Christian dating agencies. However, the options outside the Church were there. Offers had sometimes been made to them by non-Christians, but they had to decline them because of their spiritual incompatibility. They tried to express their heterosexual needs in non-erotic or non-sinful ways. That is by relating to members of the opposite sex in the Church. This was frequently misunderstood.

I have been a Christian now for twenty-two years. I have been able to experience wonderful relationships of love with other men in the Church. I have rarely been aware of misunderstandings. I do not believe I have missed out on love. I have often made mistakes – including sinful ones – and at times felt lonely, but I have never felt alone or unattached. My brother, father and mother have all died but I do not feel orphaned. There are special people in my life whom I love very much and who love me. They are a part of my life as I am of theirs. If you have been helped by anything in this book through my life it is also through their lives.

What Is Your Story?

Perhaps you are just beginning to work through the issues which caused you to buy this book? I pray that you will know God's presence with you as you do.

Maybe you are looking back at what seems like many mistakes made? May you feel a sense of their value and part in your own journey of growth.

Maybe you are struggling to understand your own sexuality? I hope the ideas and stories given have helped to clarify your self-knowledge and helped you make your own moral choices.

Perhaps your main concern is to understand the sexuality of others? I hope you have also been helped to understand yourself.

Some Recommended Reading

Dan Allender, *Bold Love* (Navpress, 1992).

Dan Allender and Tremper Longman III, *The Cry of the Soul* (Navpress, 1994).

Mario Bergner, *Setting Love in Order* (Monarch, 1995).

Andrew Comiskey, *Pursuing Sexual Wholeness* (Monarch, 1989).

Larry Crabb, *Finding God* (Zondervan/Scripture Press, 1993).

Jeanette Howard, *Out of Egypt* (Monarch, 1991).

Barbara Johnson, *Where Does a Mother Go To Resign?* (Word Books, 1994).

Thomas E. Schmidt, *Straight and Narrow* (IVP, 1995).

Elizabeth Moberly, *Homosexuality: A New Christian Ethic* (James Clarke, 1983).

John White, *Parents in Pain* (IVP, 1993).

David F. Wright, *The Christian Faith and Homosexuality* (a booklet published by Rutherford House, 1994).

Organisations

The following subscribe to the Christian basis outlined by the author:

Courage Trust, PO Box 338, Watford WD1 4BQ (0181-420-1066)

True Freedom Trust (Head Office), PO Box 3, Upton, Wirral, Merseyside L49 6NY (0151-653-0773)

Exodus International North America, PO Box 2121, San Rafael, CA 94912, USA (415-454-1017)

Exodus South Pacific, PO Box 308, Fortitude Valley, Queensland 4006, Australia (07-371-4705)

There are many secular organisations and other religious ones with a different perspective from TfT and Courage. Information about these should be obtainable from a local Gay switchboard or the Samaritans.